T0339691

HOLLYWOOD STUDIO MUSICIANS

HOLLYWOOD STUDIO MUSICIANS

Their Work and Careers in the Recording Industry

ROBERT R. FAULKNER
With a new preface by Howard S. Becker

Routledge
Taylor & Francis Group

LONDON AND NEW YORK

First published 2013 by Transaction Publishers

Published 2017 by Routledge
2 Park Square, Milton Park, Abingdon, Oxon OX14 4RN
711 Third Avenue, New York, NY 10017, USA

Routledge is an imprint of the Taylor & Francis Group, an informa business

Library of Congress Catalog Number: 2013005082

Library of Congress Cataloging-in-Publication Data

Faulkner, Robert R.
  Hollywood studio musicians : their work and careers in the recording industry / Robert R. Faulkner ; with a new preface by Howard S. Becker. -- New material this edition.
      pages cm
    1. Musicians--Employment--California--Los Angeles.
    2. Motion picture music--Production and direction--California--Los Angeles. I. Title.
ML3795.F38 2013
781.5'4202379494--dc23

                                              2013005082

ISBN 13: 978-1-4128-5253-1 (pbk)

Contents

Acknowledgments

Every author owes more debts to others than can be acknowledged, much less repaid. Among the many to whom I am grateful I would like to mention Anselm Strauss, Ralph Turner, Irving Bernstein, Gerald Platt, Oscar Grusky, David Sears, and Paul Tanner. Alexander J. Morin at Aldine Press provided invaluable suggestions and criticisms, enduring several revisions as we got the manuscript into shape. It was Strauss who initially brokered the deal on the manuscript. He read it, commented on it, and then walked it over to Howard Becker's place on Jones Street in North Beach. Howie soon wrote me a letter saying he wanted to publish it in his new "Observations" series. Thus began a long-lived collaboration of playing music and "thinking together."

For his advice and encouragement, I owe more that I can acknowledge to my advisor, colleague, and friend Raymond Murphy. He introduced me to the work of Everett C. Hughes and the Chicago style study of careers and professions. From 1965 to 1968 basic financial support was provided by a National Institute of General Medical Sciences grant to the UCLA Sociology Department. My thanks to Charles Wright, director of the program; his book on mass communications first piqued my interest in sociology.

I also would like to express my gratitude to many of the freelance musicians I interviewed—especially those with whom I had lengthy and repeated discussions. William Ulyate, Vick Arno, Gene Cipriano, Lew Kaufman, Lew Singer, Abe Most, and Dominick Fera were invaluable respondents (answering questions about their recording work and careers) and informants (sharing insights and information on the business). My initial informants urged me to "talk to those in the swim of things." I asked them who these people were and they gave me the names of musicians in the upper echelon, those on Hollywood's so called "A List." They also alerted me to the key role of contractors and composers—and the importance of their choices of musicians for film and television recording dates. Many were only too happy to share stories and fill me in on "how things work (or don't) in the business." Isn't it wonderful that people take care of us fieldworkers that way? They tell us what we should do and the trick is to learn to listen to them and do what they say. Small numbers and networks induce stories about sponsorship, status, uncertainty and honor. Thus I learned about the contingencies of high performance studio work, of contracting mechanisms in a freelance labor market, and of mobility paths into the elite 20 percent who do 80 percent of the industry's recording dates—a real life example of Pareto's power law. I also discovered that freelancers formulated a *collective perspective* on their shared problems—revolving around the dilemmas and contradictions of crisis and routine, collegiality and competition, music and money, art and commerce.

Over seventy freelance musicians helped shape the stages of my informant based data collection. I especially thank Larry Bunker, Lew Kaufman, Frank Marshall, Red Mitchell, Joachim Chassman, Mitchell Lurie, James Decker, Vincent De Rosa, Dick Nash, Sheridon Stokes, Luella Howard, and Raymond Kelley. Arthur Morton was a gracious host and introduced me to the music editors, technical staff, and orchestrators at Twentieth Century Fox Studios. I was invited to have lunch at the Fox commissary, sat at the famous "music table," where I got an ear full of the patois and humor of the profession. Personnel in the music department at Universal Studios (MCA) also gave of their time and expertise.

Many thanks to Mary Curtis and my editors at Transaction Publishers, especially Hannah Jones and Howard Schneiderman.

Finally, I owe a great deal to the percussionist Bill Goodwin, pianist Terry Trotter, composers Fred Steiner, Jerry Fielding, Dave Grusin, David Shire, Lynn Murray, trumpet artist Malcolm McNab and especially "in-house" editor and screenwriter Monica Faulkner. They know why, and that is what matters.

New Preface to the Transaction Edition
Howard S. Becker

Rob Faulkner played trumpet before he started doing sociological research. But he used his musical knowledge to do a dissertation—which led to the book you now have in your hands—on something that interested him a lot and for which he had the technical knowledge that let him do a study that was deeply knowledgeable about that subject.

The seventeen-year-old who hung around the famed Lighthouse in Hermosa Beach in Southern California, listening to the players who were inventing what came to be called West Coast jazz, went to graduate school at the University of California in Los Angeles. He learned to think of the music he was listening to and learning to play as a social product, as something that embodied the collective and cooperative activity of a lot of people. He learned to look for the forms that cooperation took and the way people learned to be part of that cooperative activity. He looked for a way to use that knowledge to do what his graduate program required of him: to do a major piece of research that would embody an *original contribution* to knowledge. I think that's the formula usually used to describe a PhD dissertation, but not many dissertations meet that standard, being original and contributing to knowledge.

Faulkner's did. He looked around the surrounding territory and realized that he wouldn't have to go far to study something that embodied all the problems he had been reading about in his classes: the structure of occupational groups, the development of

xi

occupational cultures, social stratification, the formation of collective perspectives on shared problems, the playing out of all these phenomena in individual careers as people chose paths and tried to pursue them. That something was the Hollywood studio complex, in which (among all the other things that went on in those places) musicians came together to perform and record the musical scores composers wrote as background to the films—good, bad, and indifferent—the studios produced in large quantity, year in and year out. The musicians provide an integral and necessary part of that product, but it mostly goes unnoticed by people who discuss films, knowledgeably or not, as the work of actors (all those of us who talk about seeing that great Katherine Hepburn film or Tom Cruise's newest); or the work of great directors (like the adherents of the *auteur* theory, which enshrines the film as the product of the director's vision and will); or the fewer still who, like the critic Pauline Kael, considered, perversely, that film was really a writer's medium.

Faulkner is still more likely to ask you if you have seen Quincy Jones' last film, or the wonderful one by John Williams, treating those composers as the ones who get the credit for the movies they scored. He knows better, of course, and knows that the composer is only one of the many contributors who made the film what it is (he put that knowledge to work in his later book [Faulkner 1983] on Hollywood composers, *Music on Demand*, in which he took explicitly into account the links between many of the key players in the making of a movie).

The focus on the people who recorded the background music led Faulkner to some highly *original* insights. He learned that freelance work (playing in those studio orchestras is a good example) led to a highly stratified system of professional prestige, based on the player's ability to get the job done, whatever the job was. That prestige system, in turn, governed the allocation of jobs by the people who did the hiring. This was the prototype of the now-familiar notion of the "A list"—the people employers go to first when they need some highly skilled work done—an idea Richard Caves (2000, p. 7) made good use of in his economic analysis of creative industries.

Further, Faulkner shows us how a musician's adjustment to the kind of playing and career working in the studio system provided depended in a complex way on the instrument played. Most string players had wanted to be concert soloists, but now found themselves playing uninteresting solo parts, often consisting of pages of "footballs" (that is, whole notes, an oval shape). They made a lot of money but were unhappy. Brass players and percussionists, who had for the most part come out of the world of dance bands and jazz, had far more interesting parts to play and in addition made far more money and had a far less stressful life in the studios than traveling with even the biggest names in that world had given them. They were, as a result, happy with the way their careers had turned out. That teaches us an important general sociological lesson: not to make vast sociological generalizations about things you haven't observed first-hand, like the stultifying effects of working in the "mass culture" industries, a favorite cliché of many analysts of such matters. Instead, sociologists ought to learn the details of that kind of work and see how the people who do it actually do deal with the day-to-day problems of that kind of work. Again, a highly original analysis.

Faulkner's book also embodies the most effective way to make a real *contribution* to sociological thought. He does not begin with a lengthy analysis of "theories" about "mass culture" and its baneful effects on artistic activity. Instead, he alludes to those theories but then goes directly to the far more relevant factual background of the organizational settings the artists he studied worked in. The book describes and analyzes those settings and details the kinds of perspectives and career strategies characteristic of the players who do that important support work for the movie industry. Only at the end of the book, when the reader has learned what the work really consists of, how it requires very high levels of technical skill and interpretive intelligence, does Faulkner go back to fill in the more general import of his results for an understanding of such large scale "theoretical" questions as the nature of work in mass society. The book is an object lesson to apprentice sociologists of "how to do it," how to approach general theoretical questions in a fruitful way.

So Faulkner, in his first major sociological work, produced the original contribution such work is supposed to produce. He did far more than write a good dissertation, however. He produced a sociological gem, a masterpiece of elegantly conducted field research combined with probing theoretically informed analysis, an example succeeding generations of students of the film and other creative industries have used to see "how to do it," how to do good sociology that tells us more than we knew before about some area of social life while providing clues for future investigators to apply in their own search for similar originality. Thomas Kuhn (1970, p. 52) described the study of just such examples as the way members of a scientific community learn their trade. *Hollywood Studio Musicians* perfectly exemplifies what Kuhn was talking about: a model for investigators to turn to when their own research needs help, an exemplar of how sociological research is done when it's done really well.

References

Caves, Richard E. 2000. *Creative Industries: Contracts between Art and Commerce*. Cambridge: Harvard University Press.

Faulkner, Robert. R. 1983. *Music on Demand: Composers and Careers in the Hollywood Film Industry*. New Brunswick, NJ: Transaction Publishers.

Kuhn, Thomas. 1970. *The Structure of Scientific Revolutions*. Chicago: University of Chicago Press.

CHAPTER ONE

Introduction

The film is above all a "photograph" and is already as such a technical art, with mechanical origins and aiming at mechanical repetition, in other words, thanks to the cheapness of its reproduction, a popular and fundamentally "democratic" art.

Arnold Hauser, The Social History of Art

Playing with the film track is a stiff, mechanical feeling, and I can understand why, because the composer and conductor have to catch sequences quickly on the screen. Any other way would be too expensive. What we do in one hour would probably take half a day without the click tracks . . . .It's a game, you play your part and make it come out correct, that's all.

From an interview with a bass player

To be a studio man, the ideal thing, is to do anything and everything. You play bombastic, "legit," anything . . . fight scenes, solos, all that, and really crank the stuff out. You have to have it. I'm not saying I prostitute myself, but I think you must have all the tools in order to be considered for any kind of musical situation.

From an interview with a trombone player

1

To be a successful, good musician takes a lot of skill, a lot of hard work and study, a lot of heartbreak, and a lot of disappointment. All my colleagues have these things and I know because I am one. They are talented people, very sensitive people, very hardworking people, and I have a lot of respect for them. I think they're a special breed.

From an interview with a violin player

One of the striking features of modern industrial society has been the rapid growth and development of the mass entertainment industries, based on the successful commercial application of developments in photography, film, sound recording, and other breakthroughs in electronics, chemistry, and mechanics. This is particularly apparent if we look at the size and influence of the television, motion picture, and phonograph recording industries, as indicated by the number and quality of talent recruited to them, the amount of capital investment absorbed by them, and the sophistication of their operations. These industries are unique in bringing together a combination of technological and organizational forces for the manufacture of popular entertainment. Their growth and influence has been a subject of speculation by social scientists, critics, and other observers, who have shown concern about the impact of popular culture on art and serious artists, and especially the effects of "commercialism" on writers, painters, poets, composers, and musicians—on both creative and performing artists. The mass culture industries are portrayed as assembly lines, where standardized, homogeneous products are cranked out, and profit is more important than culture, where the creator or performer is dominated by an impersonal technology and a complex production process. An artist who goes commercial is seen as selling out for the financial benefits of well paid, but alienating employment; he is seen as allowing his unique talents to be undermined by an industry geared toward the public, the mass audience, rather than toward culture-bearing elites.

Curiously enough, discussion about persons employed in the popular-culture and mass-communications industries has resulted in many dry remarks but little careful understanding of these settings. Indeed, research is exceedingly slim. Powdermaker's work on Hollywood is dated and concerns only the most visible segment of the motion picture industry—the directors, producers, and actors. Huaco's recent book is a discussion of styles of film, but it does not provide a systematic treatment of the production personnel who make them; however, some of this information can be found in Rosten's saga of the movie colony. Nash's article on the composer contains some ideas about commercialism and the creative artist, but his remarks are brief and not presented in detail, nor does he describe how composers actually go about their work in the commercial scene. No studies have extended Griff's ideas about commercial artists to other work settings and occupations. While Becker offers insights into the career contingencies and motivation for "going commercial" in his articles on dance musicians, his analysis concerns mainly performers working on casual jobs and in night clubs rather than in the mass-media industries. Important leads about symphony musicians' definition of career success, feeling of entrapment, and alternative career lines are suggested in Westby's interviews with these performers. Most sociologists have overlooked the mass-culture industries as work settings; they have preferred to focus on the media content rather than on its employees, or on the art of popular entertainment rather than on the artists, performers, and technicians who shape it.[1]

In the absence of information, students interested in this aspect of society have been prone to rely on speculation. Much has been written about a so-called cultural elite who operate within "some aesthetic or literary tradition." These are "top men in the sphere of . . . aesthetics and entertainment, who carry the core values and standards of the sphere and serve as models for those working in it." "Mass pressures" in "mass society" bring about a destruction of this elite and its artistic values; the debilitation of culture is one result, and the erosion of elite values another.[2] Other critics see the mass media as staffed by "anti-intellectual intellectuals" and creative hacks, driven by grubby materialism, who turn out our films, television programs, records, and magazines. Many recognize these

1. Hortense Powdermaker, *Hollywood: The Dream Factory* (Boston: Little, Brown, and Company, 1950); George A. Huaco, *The Sociology of Film Art* (New York: Basic Books, 1965); Leo Rosten, *Hollywood: The Movie Colony, The Movie Makers* (New York: Harcourt, Brace and Company, Inc., 1941); Dennison Nash, "The Alienated Composer," in *The Arts in Society,* Robert N. Wilson (ed.), (Englewood Cliffs, N.J.: Prentice-Hall, 1964), pp. 37–60; Mason Griff, "The Commercial Artist: A Study in Changing and Consistent Identities," in Maurice Stein, et al. (eds.), *Identity and Anxiety; Survival of the Person in Mass Society* (New York: Free Press, 1960), pp. 219–241; Howard Becker, *The Outsiders* (New York: Free Press, 1963), pp. 70–100, pp. 101–119; David Westby, "The Career Experiences of the Symphony Orchestra Musician," *Social Forces* 38 (December, 1960), 223–230.

2. For a review of this literature see Herbert J. Gans, "Popular Culture in America: Social Problem in a Mass Society or Social Asset in a Pluralistic Society?" in *Social Problems: A Modern Approach,* edited by Howard Becker (New York: Wiley, 1966), pp. 549–620; Arnold Hauser, *The Social History of Art* (New York: Vintage Books, 1951, Volumes I-IV); Bernard Rosenberg and Norris Fliegel, *The Vanguard Artist: Portrait and Self Portrait* (Chicago: Quadrangle Books, 1965).

views as overdrawn, and some realize that they may be highly romantic. But these models of mass culture have a polemical value: they are perspectives on what culture should be and what artists should do, based on what these critics think was true in the past. The past is easy to romanticize, but it is perhaps too easy to judge the current scene by these ideal standards.

While I share some of these concerns about "culture," my perspective is different. A reader interested in the "debilitation of artists in mass society" might consider personal alienation and "artistic integrity" to be key problems. Another might see conforming to the tastes of the audience, "the democratic mass of media consumers," as the most important problem faced by commercial artists. Others may wish to compare the man on the assembly line with the artist in the mass-media industry. These are important problems, but they are also highly evaluative standpoints. I propose that much of the behavior of creative and performing artists in mass media setting can be viewed as *work*. They write, perform, and produce in highly organized teams that demand coordination; they face routine work pressures, try to handle mistakes at work, control the activities of colleagues, and cope with the risks of personal failure. The structure of work itself and routine work problems faced by these talented individuals as employees are the points I wish to emphasize.

This emphasis raises several concrete questions: What is the precise impact of employment in the mass-media industries on a group of skilled artists? How do they look at their work? Do they see it as giving them opportunities to use and express their talents, and, if so, under what conditions? What is the relationship between their careers and their employment in highly technical and organized production organizations? Is the artist directly influenced by the social setting, by what he brings to the setting, or by his career aspirations? Is there something unique about artists employed in these industries, and, indeed, what are the particular characteristics of these individuals? Answers to these questions involve an exploration and detailed analysis of the commercial work setting, work problems, and careers of those who conceive, produce, and perform mass-media fare. I have chosen performing studio musicians (studio work is all inclusive; it includes motion picture and television film jobs, live and tape TV, record dates, and radio and television jingles) because they represent a unique combination of artistic talent, long training, and perfected skills located in a highly industrial and complex production process.

These performers who work in the Los Angeles recording studios are anachronistic in our age of large-scale industrial organizations. They own their instruments; their skills cannot be acquired in a short time, and years of training and persistent practice are required; and their talents are not widely usable outside the music scene. They come from a wide variety of career settings: jazz groups, big bands, symphony orchestras, the concert stages, and other types of musical jobs. In the mass-media industries, their role is only one part of a production process which is collective to an unusual extent. Film production, as an example, develops through three phases: pre-production and planning (involving producers, directors, casting directions, production managers), production and filming (involving actors, directors, cameramen, and all of the people associated with the actual filming), and post-production or final assembly. The musician enters only at this last stage, when the film is edited, special effects and the sound track are added, and the music score is composed, arranged, and timed to precisely match the film action. It is at this point that the musicians are hired. Thus, the composer, conductors, music editor, arranger, and performer comprise only one of several specialized production units. The musical underscore is subsidiary to dialogue, sound effects, and film action; and while soundtrack albums and movie themes have become important elements in the sales of films, music is essentially an adjunct to the film. It is geared to the film medium; pace, timing, dynamics, and phrasing follow the screen action. In contrast to chamber music, jazz, rock, or orchestral music, film music itself is not the thing. It comes at the end of the film assembly—after writing, casting, scripts, sets, makeup, costumes, dubbing, editing, and a host of other jobs.

Despite the assembly-line nature of motion picture, television film, and phonograph record dates, each score is unique. Melody, rhythm, harmony, orchestration, length of individual takes, and difficulty of parts vary with each film. This inherent variety in studio work requires musicians to be prepared for uncertainty. They always have something new to play, someone new to play under, and they must be on top of their musical skills all the time. On studio dates (and even on the same date) musicians find a wide variety of scores, from rock to jazz-oriented compositions to lush, symphonic music. The folklore of the studios is full of rich anecdotes about the abilities of performers to play anything at sight, in any style, to follow any conductor no matter what his abilities, and do this efficiently, with precise intonation, phrasing, and attack.

In the world of the studio musician a set of routine problems is generated that must be negotiated, handled, and rendered as predictable or manageable as possible. From the everyday viewpoint of these musicians, one persistent problem centers around the *control* they have over the conditions of work: the composers and conductors they play under, the studios they perform in, the colleagues they work with. Another problem is tied to their *skills* and musical talents: misuse and under-use of abilities in studio work, performing under imposing technological conditions, uncertainty about which skills will be demanded from day to day, and the fluctuation between routine and crisis at work. A third is the level of personal *honor* claimed and socially accorded by colleagues, one's position in the studio pecking order, and one's perception of being "inside" or "outside" influential circles. Recurrent work problems also revolve around the *market situation* of the individual performer in the occupation and that of the occupation in the industry: the structure and intensity of competition for scarce jobs and monetary rewards, the fluctuations in music budgets in mass-media production, and the consequences of greater consumer demand for these entertainments. These concrete work problems constitute a set of interrelated contingencies upon which the studio musician's work and career depend; they are key features to which he must attend. This occupation must be analyzed (1) in terms of the structural context in which these problems occur, (2) from the cognitive perspective of the musician and his definitions of their relative importance, and (3) in terms of their impact on his work experience.

Work problems have theoretical relevance in linking the social situation of an occupation to the person. This identification of the individual with his occupation is best seen in the professions where, as Hughes puts it, "the culture and technique, the etiquette and skill appear in the individual as personal traits." Culture and shared perspectives arise in response to some set of problems faced by occupational members; they constitute taken-for-granted understandings for dealing with skill, control over work, status, and market situation. These understandings are reflected in the attitudes and behavior of the individual, and they shape his inner experience. A major part of the culture of a work group, then, consists of organized solutions to these taken-for-granted problems, strains, and tensions.[3]

Occupational members also bring experiences, identities, and perspectives with them from other settings. They hold ideas and values which are derived from previous occupations; they carry understandings with them from other stages of their career. The expectations, wants, and tensions people bring to their work should be treated as a major variable when we look at how they view their present jobs.[4] The meaning a man finds in his work and the problems that are part of his cognitive perspective are anchored not only in the technical and social organization of work, but also in his prior career experiences. The link between work problems and personality, occupational structure, and inner experience is not automatic. To examine work perspectives, I have chosen to explore the career lines which lead persons out of one setting and into another. My working hypothesis is that the actor's own definition of his career can be regarded theoretically as

3. Everett Cherrington Hughes, *Men and Their Work* (Glencoe, Ill: Free Press, 1958); C. Wright Mills, *White Collar* (New York: Oxford University Press, Galaxy Books, 1956). My particular debt to the writings of Hughes should be evident throughout this book.
4. For a discussion of prior orientations, "latent identities," and their theoretical importance, see Howard Becker and Blanche Geer, "Latent Culture: A Note on the Theory of Latent Social Roles," *Administrative Science Quarterly* 5 (September, 1960), 304–313; John H. Goldthorpe, David Lockwood, Frank Bechhofer, and Jennifer Platt, *The Affluent Worker: Industrial Attitudes and Behavior* (London: Cambridge University Press, 1968).

mediating between the objective work setting and his subjective work experiences.

A distinction between work problems in specific settings and career problems throughout the individual's entire work history is more important in occupations where people undergo long and difficult training before entering the world of work. Hughes notes that, "in general, we may say that the longer and more rigorous the period of initiation into an occupation, the more culture and technique are associated with it, and the more deeply impressed are its attitudes upon the person." A performing musician's training, for example, is extremely long, most often beginning very early in life, and the social context in which he learns and performs (his role models, repertoire, and personal success) awakens desires for artistic fulfillment and creativity in work—values often forgotten, ignored, or even not defined as relevant by many professionals and white-collar employees.

The realities of making a living in music constitute a major set of career and work problems.[5] These realities often conflict with the ideals that first encouraged the player to undergo the rigors of discipline and practice, as well as the values on which his aspirations are based. The fracture between dream and reality seems particularly severe for those who are taught one set of values in their training and who then, in due course during their careers, find that these cannot possibly be fulfilled if they are to earn a living. As a major source of conflict and a matter of compromise, the way in which performing and creative artists deal with this fracture is of considerable practical

5. For a review of this literature see William J. Baumol and William G. Bowen, *Performing Arts: The Economic Dilemma* (New York: Twentieth Century Fund, 1966); Samuel Antek, *This Was Toscanini* (New York: Vanguard Press, 1963), especially pp. 71–74.

and theoretical importance. Musicians working in the Hollywood recording studios represent one example of this dilemma between ideals and the system of social interaction in which the occupational role is performed. My research is based on the different meanings that members attach to their career actions, and whether and under what structural conditions these interpretations influence the perspectives they have of their work.

Market Setting

The business of music constitutes no homogeneous grouping of performers about whose characteristics one can easily summarize. The profession can be viewed in terms of its segmental features: there is a wide array of working settings, many career escalators, and diverse identities. Even within the same metropolitan area, the number of musical subcommunities or orbits varies in terms of complexity of production process and managerial organization, stability of work, size of enterprise, artistic and financial ends, colleagues, and ideologies. While the description of this complex and its impact on musicians would make an interesting study itself, the remainder of this chapter will be devoted to a brief outline of the commercial recording centers in this country, placing the Los Angeles studios and their performers in a broader context. The economic and employment setting of symphony orchestras will be discussed as a context for comparison. Later chapters will attempt to portray the wider pattern of work settings using career lines to reveal their structure and bearing on studio musicians' decisions to go commercial. Such a selection of materials is necessary because the primary interest here is the system of studio work. Nevertheless, practical reasons lie behind this presentation. Neither the local musicians' unions nor the Census provide detailed statistics of these different segments of work, aggregate number of union members employed, or continuity of employment. The New York local, for example, is comprised of 32,000 members, and the Los Angeles local has more than 18,000; lumped together in these figures are orchestral, jazz, and studio pros who earn their livelihood as full-time players, and amateurs who have a union card and play on weekends for a few dollars. The job of locating, sifting out, and comparing the work and careers of the wide range of musicians, their types of employment, and behavior patterns is left for other investigators.

The kind of career a musician is likely to have and the degree of success enjoyed is contingent on the structure of available opportunities, the market demand for his services, and, correspondingly, the unpredictability and changeability of this market as it is affected by shifts in consumer wants and preferences. These are conditions surrounding an occupation that are decisive for the success of the performer. These macroscopic aspects direct our attention to the kinds of work settings and institutions in which careers move.

Some of the most complete information about performing "classical" musicians is found in the reports of The American Symphony Orchestra League (ASOL). The League classifies orchestras into four main groupings based on size of annual budgets. The best established and oldest orchestras have annual budgets in excess of $500,000. In the twenty-five major symphonies a great deal of diversity exists in levels of remuneration, length of seasonal schedules, and numbers employed. Sizes of the orchestras range from 80 to 110; some have seasons of 30 or fewer weeks, and in the mid-sixties the annual pay in five of the majors was around $3,000.[6] The image of the orchestra world is dominated by the five illustrious organizations — Cleveland, New York, Chicago, Boston, and Philadelphia — where 52-week seasons are now guaranteed, and this guarantee will take effect in Cincinnati in the 1970's. The recent contract negotiated in Kansas City elevated the season from 20 weeks in 1969–70 to 34 in 1970-71. The Boston Symphony, for example, employs more than 100 musicians, and in 1970 guarantees them a base scale of $14,500 per year plus $1,000 from recordings. They have a 31-week symphony season with a one-week paid vacation, a nine-week pop season, and an eight-week summer season with a four-week paid vacation. In other orchestras musicians and union representatives claim that even with longer seasons and higher salaries, their earnings are below other professionals. In Rochester, the minimum annual earnings are around $7,500 a season and in Indianapolis $5,700 a season.[7]

The annual budgets of metropolitan orchestras range from $100,000 to $250,000. Typically located in urban areas of less than half a million people, there are more than 45 such organizations comprised of amateurs and professionals with a total of approximately 3,500 performers (listed in the ASOL findings in *Musical America,* 1966). Considerably more than 500 orchestras can be classified as urban by the League in terms of budgets ranging from $50,000 to $100,000, and the number of musicians playing in them totals about 6,000. As Baumol and Bowen point out, some of these orchestras are professional or quasi-professional in character, comprised of amateurs with a core unit of professionals picked up for the final set of rehearsals and performance. They estimate

6. Baumol and Bowen, p. 17; *International Musician,* May, 1961.
7. *New York Times,* March 10, 1970, p. 50.

that fewer than twenty per cent of the members are re-
munerated for the performance. And finally, community
orchestras operate much like their urban counterparts,
except their budgets are less than $50,000; there are
nearly a thousand such amateur and quasi-professional
groups throughout the country.

The opera setting is strikingly similar. While according
to *Opera News* there were more than 750 opera-
producing organizations in this country giving approximately 4,000 performances during the 1958-59 season,
few are continually operating and few provide opportunities for operatic careers. Dominating the scene are the
four leading theaters employing from 80 to 120 instrumentalists: the Metropolitan Opera, the New York
City Opera, the San Francisco Opera, and the Chicago
Lyric Opera. The Met's management, orchestra, and New
York Local 802 recently negotiated a contract that provided for raising salaries to $300 a week, increased re-
hearsal scales, shorter work week, and more pay for
weekly radio broadcasts. This orchestra now has the top
scale salary in the classical field.

Outside of the "legitimate" orbit of symphony orchestras and opera companies resides the multi-million dollar
world of commercial music. In terms of industrial organization, production, marketing, distribution, and expenditures for composers and performers, three commercial centers dominate this separate musical world
—New York, Nashville, and Los Angeles. Everyone is
exposed daily to the work of these musicians. Their writing and playing can be heard on television and radio
commercial jingles, on film sound tracks, and on phonograph recordings. Little is known about these musicians
outside of their own industry, despite a steady stream of
underscores and backings for films; soft-drink, airline,

cigarette, and automobile commercials; and rhythm-and-blues, country and western, and pop groups. With the exception of composers and conductors, the performers only rarely find their names on record jackets and are infrequently seen by audiences or eventual consumers of their work, except occasionally on some network television shows which use big bands.

In terms of technical prowess, sight reading ability, and the amount of money they make per year, these studio performers are regarded as the elite commercial musicians in the country. Interviews with performers, composers, and union personnel who work in these three centers indicate that although there are thousands of players in the union and many hundreds of talented professionals in each city, there are only a few hundred studio pros. In New York a core group of 300 are consistently called for high paying record dates ($85 for a minimum three-hour call) and jingles ($40 an hour plus residuals). Estimates were that in the late sixties more than 40 studios in New York equipped for commercial production made more than fifty per cent of all TV spot commercials. Many of the highly demanded studio pros comprise the core of 105 performers on the staff at three major networks. Outside the circle of high-paying studio and recording work, the Broadway and off-Broadway pit orchestras employ anywhere from five to 30 musicians, depending on the nature of the shows, and use a total of about 400 players throughout the year. Fifty men are on staff at Radio City Music Hall, with 30 substitutes on call.

Nashville is the center of country-and-western recording, publishing, and production. It is a major studio center for rhythm and blues (r and b), Top 40, gospel, and country recording dates. The home of numerous song-writers and performers, more than 600 artists are under

contract to record in Nashville. Major companies with
production facilities are RCA, Columbia, Monument,
MCA, Capitol, Decca, Stop, and Chart. Acuff-Rose, one
of the dominant publishing companies in the world, has its
headquarters there. In 1969 more than 3,000 records, 100
commercial jingles, and several television programs were
made in the studios.[8] While the number of performing
musicians is of course smaller than can be found on either
coast, a pattern of selective demand for a core of studio
pros is evident. It is estimated that about 40 players do
the majority of recording backings and underscores. The
basic rate for their work is $86.00 for a three-hour master
session. At this rate, a top-caliber studio musician in
Nashville, New York, or Los Angeles, who is in demand
by leaders, artists-singers, composers-arrangers, and
other studio personnel can make from $20,000 to $80,000
a year.

Contrasted with these commercial centers of activity
are several metropolitan orbits. Detroit and Chicago are
middle-ground record studio centers; Memphis has
recently expanded to approximately 10 studios and is one
of the top four producers of country, r and b, and gospel
recordings; Dallas is growing as a center for TV and radio
jingles; Bakersfield, California is the home of Blue Book
and Owen publishing houses, several record labels, and an
active studio scene; Toronto is the major center for record
and jingle production in Canada. Las Vegas, emerging as
a market producer due to recordings of shows, also employs several hundred players for its theaters, casinos, and
smaller clubs. In the San Francisco Bay area the rock
scene is shaped by about 150 rock bands and several new

8. AFM, Nashville Local Report; see *Billboard,* January 10, 1970,
March 7, 1970.

studios with numerous record companies: Fantasy, Capitol, Vanguard, ABC, Epic, Columbia, Acta/Dot, Rca, and the Mercury family.

In Los Angeles the studio recording setting is different from these various middle-ground orbits and the two production centers of New York and Nashville. In the music business on the East Coast, the jingle, phonograph, and network recording jobs stand at the top of the occupational hierarchy in terms of money, colleagues, and preferred hours. In Hollywood the motion picture and television film and phonograph recording studios dominate the scene. And this setting has an active network production output—the majority of taped television variety shows, not including late-night talk shows, originates from downtown Hollywood or Burbank. In terms of basic earnings of musicians in studio work the film studios are first, followed by the recording sector. Twentieth Century-Fox, Universal Pictures (part of MCA), Warner Brothers (Kinney National Service), Disney, Metro-Goldwyn-Mayer, ABC Pictures Corporation (ABC-owned), Cinema Center Films (CBS-owned), and a larger number of independent producers stand at the top of the studio structure. A closely interconnected orbit contains the large recording companies with studios and production headquarters in Hollywood: Columbia, RCA, Capitol, Liberty, World Pacific, MGM, and Decca. These companies are among the top producers of rock, rhythm and blues, pop, and country-pop styles.

In the 1963-64 television season, the Hollywood studios produced a significant proportion of network prime-time shows, more than sixty-seven per cent of the 88 shows. Twenty of ABC's shows in 1964 were made either by the studios themselves or as associates with a growing number of independent film makers; CBS had approximately 22 programs; and NBC, about 17. In 1967 Fox Studios was producing 11 series; Universal, 9; followed by Paramount-Desilu, Warners, and others.

A nucleus of 300 studio performers comprise the highly demanded musicians doing almost all of the work in films, records, and commercial transcriptions or jingles. Basic scale earnings of all musicians, composers, arrangers, and other staff are extremely lucrative. In 1967 earnings from television jingles alone were more than $400,000. Musicians playing television film calls for the major studios and independents (who use the major facilities most often) earned nearly $3,800.000. Motion picture calls, next to jingles the most lucrative type of three-hour studio call, amounted to $3,000,000 in basic scale for musicians and staff.[9]

Those highly in demand, moreover, can frequently bargain for double scale (over $150 a call) or scale and a half. It is ironic that the earnings of these studio pros in 1967 for TV jingles nearly equals the combined support given the Denver, San Francisco, Cincinnati, National Symphony, and Buffalo Philharmonic orchestras by the Government's National Endowment for the Arts in 1970.[10]

A variety of unpredictable and uncertain conditions grows out of the nature of film, record, and jingle production in the Hollywood studios. At the risk of some over-simplification, the job market can be characterized as inherently changing, where top management and the heads of studios respond to shifts in consumer demand, fads in styles of production, and the economic constraints im-

---

9. AFM, Local 47 report. This figure includes leaders, contractors, arrangers, copyists, and performing instrumentalists.
10. *New York Times,* March 9, 1970.

posed by competitive markets and a cost-controlled business world.

The return investments for Hollywood film makers and the studios center around box-office receipts; production expenses are large and can be recovered only by attracting large audiences. The informal economic guideline is that a picture must gross two and a half times its production cost to break even. Thus a 10- or 15-million dollar flop has serious consequences for the studio's operating budget and the success of the enterprise. For example, MGM and Paramount are attempting to enforce a two-million dollar budget limit on productions. Television, highpriced stars, slow response to changing audience demands, and highly expensive (and risky) blockbusters have all contributed to the economic problems of the major studios. In 1969 five of the seven major studios were in the red, losing more than $100 million dollars; box-office gross was nearly twenty-five per cent less than in the mid-forties; and production was down from the schedule of 40 or more films during those days to around 10 to 20 in 1970.

For television film makers, the networks and advertisers comprise the demand or consumer market. The price is determined by what a sponsor will pay to the television networks for the potential audience attracted by a series, a special, or other type of show. NBC, CBS, and ABC, for example, sell air time to advertisers who aim to attract a market through the stations' affiliates. The affiliates clear or set aside time, and the prime hours are between seven and ten P.M. Television is advertising-oriented, and the buyers' expenditures, like the mass-consumer expenditures for motion pictures, are extremely important for the networks, stations, production studios who supply the shows, and their staff. Made at a great deal of cost, pilot films for TV can run into many thousands of dollars (one way of spreading studio risk is to make two-hour pilots that can be run as movies). When a series for television is sold, the sponsor has the prerogative of cancelling his commitment after a certain number of weeks have elapsed into the season. Ratings, media research, and audits provide the major cues for the audience acquired. The bi-weekly Nielsen sample ratings, the effect of these ratings on advertisers, and the impact of the advertisers on all involved in production and distribution cause much uncertainty for the studios and network. If the show receives low audience ratings, sponsors will typically cancel their option. If the option is not picked up, production of the show is stopped, and the network looks for another show to take its place.

Several conditions are decisive for the work and careers of studio performers. The following are illustrative contingencies which directly impinge on the performer and deserve comment:

1. Record, film, and jingle companies operate in a competitive environment. The foregoing has been an attempt to portray the external features of that system. Studios in various commercial orbits differ in their economic profit margins, product demand, cost structures, and allocation of budgets for particular stages of the production process. Hollywood's complex of recording studios are in competition, openly or not, with other metropolitan centers of commercial productions. Moreover, within the confines of the Los Angeles scene, studios are in competition with one another. The volume and type of work for the isolated player are determined by a complex of managerial decisions and activities largely beyond his control. Runaway productions, films scored and performed in Europe, the attempts of New York City government to attract film

makers, and the rumored shifting of some record and jingle work from New York to Los Angeles illustrates the problems of external contingencies.

2. Within the local Hollywood setting, a market economy of studio work translates music and musicians into their dollars-and-cents equivalents. Music departments must compete with other production staffs for the budget, and can be cut or expanded by the calculus of organizational decisions. Cost structures directly influence expenditures for composers and conductors, the number of players hired for the call, amount of rehearsal and recording time, and the care which goes into recording, editing, and dubbing after the musicians play under the microphones and the package is assembled.

3. The unpredictability of the mass-media market and its susceptibility to consumer and audience behavior generates (a) extreme sensitivity to cost considerations on the part of management, and (b) alertness to the impact of these external constraints on the work situation of studio musicians. Some examples are useful here. First, a popular spy series on television a few years ago was budgeted in such a way that set designs and tricky explosions absorbed much of the studio's outlay. The music budget was cut to absorb these costs, and the proposed orchestra was slashed to under six studio men. Second, composers and television producers found that four or five celli produce the same richness of tone that once required a violin and viola section of at least ten players. The argument was that a three-inch television speaker reproduced a few celli better than many violins. In the late sixties, many violin players found themselves getting fewer and fewer TV calls. Third, a new generation of studio composers, many with jazz and big-band backgrounds, are writing pop, jazz-oriented, and rock scores for television, records, and

films. One implication of this is that flexible jazz-oriented musicians, often armed with electronic instruments, are doing increasingly more work. Fourth, motion picture sound-track albums are beginning to hit the top of industry sales charts. Independent producers, as well as the large studio management, are finding that increasing emphasis on music in films pays off; cost factors now often take into account the composer along with the star, writer, and director, thereby upgrading the role of music and musicians. A counter-trend, however, can be seen in the use on film soundtracks of rock and pop groups already recorded on discs, thereby bypassing the film studio and its performers.

4. Hiring of musicians is done on a free-lance basis. There are no contract or staff orchestras, and a musician's security in this fluctuating market environment is dependent upon how he fits into the formal and informal social organization of studio work. (The next chapter deals with this in detail). The contract studio orchestra operated from 1944 to 1957, when negotiations between the union local and studios fell through and open hiring for film work began. This original contract set prescriptions for a minimum number of musicians to be employed by each studio on an annual basis, a certain number of guaranteed hours per year for which the musician would be paid, and several stipulations concerning the working conditions for these "studio musicians." In 1946 Metro-Goldwyn-Mayer, Twentieth Century-Fox, and Warner Brothers agreed to employ 50 musicians each on the yearly contract basis. Paramount contracted 45 players for its orchestra; and Columbia, RKO Radio Pictures, Republic Productions, and Universal agreed to 36 musicians each on the guaranteed annual salary basis. The contract was extended for a year in 1948 and renewed again in 1949

and 1951; at the beginning of 1952 it was renegotiated for a two-year period with a 15 per cent wage increase in that year and a 5 per cent increase in 1954. In addition to the eight major studios, the industry contained a large number of independent producers. Four groups of independents were formed. One group agreed to employ 40 performers on an annual basis. These musicians could be used by all members of the group. The other three agreed to employ 20 men each. Musicians could work only for companies which had signed contracts with the American Federation of Musicians (AFM).

Some of the market contingencies are indicated in the following tables. Table 1.1 shows the basic scale earnings and the number of musicians under contract during the period of 1951 through the end of the contracts. Although the musicians' income remained stable, the actual number of hours worked declined — reflecting the decreasing production of films by the studios. For instance, MGM guaranteed its musicians 26,000 hours per year through the fifties but in 1956 actually "used up" only slightly over 47 per cent of those hours, as compared to over 90 per cent used in 1954. Warner Brothers, after employing its musicians 23,684 hours in 1954 (or 91 per cent of the guaranteed work hours) dropped to 18,895 hours three years later.

Indicative of this decrease in film hours for musicians was the fact that negotiations between the studios and AFM began to deteriorate as film companies refused to agree to wage increases. Pointing to their falling net profits, sagging box office receipts, and decreasing film releases, the companies terminated their contracts in 1958.

At approximately this time, a series of political moves were being made by musicians in AFM, Local 47, to

Table 1.1. Musicians' Earnings in the Major Motion Picture Contract Orchestras: 1951–1957*
(in thousands of dollars)

	(number employed)	1951	1952	1953	1954	1955	1956	1957
Columbia	(36)†	290	327	329	336	338	343	343
Fox	(50)	339	449	449	465	472	476	481
MGM	(50)	399	456	464	482	482	484	483
Paramount	(45)	355	369	372	384	388	386	387
RKO	(36)	253	289	295	–	–	–	–
Republic	(36)	257	284	286	194	187	187	–
Universal	(36)	263	304	306	318	321	322	322
Warner Bros	(50)	406	454	451	464	465	465	465

* Adapted from AFM, Local 47, tax report. These figures do not include contractors, arrangers, and copyists; only in-strumentalists on contract at the studios are listed above.
† Number in parenthesis is the size of orchestra under contract signed by the studio and the Federation.

rescind the power of union leader James Petrillo and to remove collective bargaining with the film studios from the control of Local 47's leadership. Among the many issues which created this conflict was the AFM's rulings under Petrillo which placed a percentage of the wages earned by recording musicians directly into the Musicians' Trust Fund. Desiring more local autonomy, control over their wages, and better conditions of studio work, some musicians filed suit against Petrillo. Partially because of their impatience with moderates who desired to put pressure on Petrillo by working through the existing leadership and partially due to their effective political leverage, the Musicians Guild of America, headed by Cecil Reed, was certified by the National Labor Relations Board to represent studio musicians in their negotiations with the film industry. From 1958 to 1960 the Guild represented this segment of the Local. In 1960 the membership voted to return to the AFM rather than the Guild.

Table 1.2 shows the total basic scale earnings for musical production personnel at six film studios from 1961 to 1967. The contingencies which free-lance musicians face are reflected in the year-to-year fluctuations of earnings, particularly in comparison with the contract orchestras (Table 1.1), and the differential distribution of these earnings by these studios. Twentieth Century-Fox, for instance, after a sharp decline in motion picture production in 1962 and 1963, began to re-emerge as a leading producer of television film in 1965. Warner Brothers' scale payments to musical personnel were largely for motion picture work, as apparently little television film work was done at that studio. Universal and Fox show the largest payments to musicians in both film areas, in some cases $250,000 to $300,000 more than the other studios. Obviously musicians "on call" at these studios occupy an economically desirable position in the free-lance hiring system.

Table 1.2. Total Basic Scale Earnings for Musicians in Six Film Studios: 1961–1967*
(in dollars)

	1961		1962		1963		1964	
	Motion Picture	TV Films	Motion Picture	TV Films	Motion Picture	TV Films	Motion Picture	TV Films
Columbia	208,124	264,393	234,632	367,539	92,950	267,029	215,817	126,281
Walt Disney	153,334	112,960	97,877	131,021	351,936	78,268	82,747	133,615
20th Century-Fox	360,666	229,177	158,192	70,204	296,439	19,877	367,012	256,983
MGM	280,659	130,062	540,200	217,107	372,154	321,788	318,299	279,779
Paramount	318,341	0	273,563	0	321,137	0	176,047	0
Warner Brothers	288,392	156,242	310,993	129,784	399,934	88,172	208,627	0

	1965		1966		1967	
	Motion Picture	TV Films	Motion Picture	TV Films	Motion Picture	TV Films
Columbia	148,016	321,167	358,154	231,258	338,637	171,059
Walt Disney	101,503	103,946	233,533	122,741	261,120	177,117
20th Century-Fox	221,832	663,068	338,624	870,000	490,965	534,134
MGM	494,072	342,734	398,275	320,986	267,782	118,905
Paramount	288,162	0	286,699	0	190,845	0
Warner Brothers	255,062	244,140	338,224	132,766	400,689	80,276
Universal	310,360	500,569	399,342	600,864	480,554	537,063

* Adapted from AFM, Local 47, tax report. These figures are earnings according to the basic union scale; they do not include over scale payments. (Includes leaders, contractors, arrangers, copyists, and instrumentalists.)

Table 1.3. Total Basic Scale Earnings by Type of Production: 1961–1967*
(in dollars)

	1961	1962	1963	1964	1965	1966	1967
Motion Pictures (Major Studios)	1,652,750	1,625,467	1,855,143	1,614,381	1,819,009	2,352,855	2,430,594
Motion Picture (Independent Studios)	677,884	592,648	1,114,079	714,035	552,797	579,725	577,621
Total	2,330,634	2,218,115	2,969,222	2,328,416	2,371,806	2,932,580	3,008,215
Television Films	2,304,687	2,365,751	2,469,917	2,911,226	3,757,217	3,854,058	3,796,606
Television Commercials	291,617	285,791	356,671	347,671	353,993	426,717	419,625

* Adapted from AFM, Local 47, tax report. Includes leaders, contractors, arrangers, copyists, and instrumentalists.

Table 1.3 shows the impact of television film on the overall earnings of musicians. The major studios and independents combined had higher overall payments to musical personnel than their payments in motion pictures since 1964. This reflects the basic structural change within the industry's type of production as well as an upturn in the level of earnings for free-lance musicians since 1961. This table also indicates a strong and consistent rise in earnings from television commercials.

Again it should be emphasized that not every studio fully entered into this general increase in earnings, nor that the performers who were under contract moved easily into the free-lance system. Although we have pointed to a rise in musicians' earnings since the early sixties, not all were fortunate enough to participate in these new sources of income. Some were displaced as their "home" studio failed to maintain their "first call" agreement. Others were forced outside as studios cut back and orchestras were reduced in size. Still others were unable to compete successfully either on the basis of their skills or because of their lack of prestige within the occupation.

The career of a free-lancer, with its yearly fluctuations, unpredictability, and sudden jolts in volume and types of work, is likely to depend on a variety of problematic conditions: the overall economic performance of the Los Angeles studios; fads in audiences preferences for films, records, and mass-media fare; the impact of managerial decisions on the use of music and performers; negotiations between union and industry; and how the performers fits into the stratification system of the occupation.

The description and analysis in this study are based on fifteen months of interviewing and field work from the summer of 1966 to the fall of 1967. The methods of our research and the criteria for selecting our respondents developed as the field work progressed. Certain problems had to be solved, such as gaining access to these musicians, defining and redefining the substantive problems to be investigated, working and re-working the interview schedule, and building up comparisons within the occupation. For a discussion of the sample and methods, refer to Methodological Appendixes A and B. These sections set forth the final methods and techniques employed, the sample, and its characteristics, with a personal account of the research and some reflections on the investigation.

The Hollywood Studio Scene and the Free-Lance Musician

The role of music and musicians in the Hollywood motion picture, television film, and recording studios may be examined from several related perspectives: (1) the technical operations employed in film making, (2) the way in which these operations are assigned and the resulting division of studio labor, and (3) the hiring of musicians in the free-lance market. These features of technology and work organization illustrate the importance of production pressures in understanding musicians' attitudes and feelings about their work.[1] Like the work of SAC bomber pilots, technicians at Cape Kennedy, air-traffic controllers, and railroad dispatchers, the structure of the studio setting is

1. The link between technology, work structure, and inner experience is a central focus of the work of William Foote Whyte, Charles R. Walker, and Robert Blauner. See Walker's *Modern Technology and Civilization* (New York: McGraw-Hill Book Co., 1962) for a review of this field, and Blauner's *Alienation and Freedom* (Chicago: University of Chicago Press, 1964).

an intimately subdivided, elaborately coordinated, and precisely timed activity.

The studio is fundamentally a big business which uses assembly-line methods for the production of film.[2] Work schedules follow the chronological order of the film making, from screen writing, to shooting, to editing, to the assembly of film and sound on the reel. These operations require the technical and creative services of such diverse departments as casting, production staff, construction, special effect, lighting, sound recording, editing, etc. There are two types of music for television film, motion pictures, and TV commercials. The first is music at the *pre-production* stage, written before the film is shot. These recordings are played back while the scenes are actually being filmed, producing precise synchronization of lip movements and dramatic action. Pre-recording for dubbings of this type are imprinted onto or "laid in" with the film scenes at the final stage of assembly. This technique is also used where pre-recorded or "canned" music is used, that is, music not specifically written for the film or TV series. It is also employed where former sound tracks for TV films are reissued or reused (called "tracking"). The second type of screen music is written and recorded at the *post-production* stage of assembly; it is the process we will be more concerned with because it is used most often and dramatizes the role of film music composed especially for foreground action and dialogue.

In the economic organization of film personnel, composers, arrangers, conductors, and performing musicians typically account for only three to six per cent of the total

2. Hortense Powdermaker makes this analogy between movie making and the assembly line explicit in *Stranger and Friend: The Way of an Anthropologist* (New York: W.W. Norton, 1966), p. 217; Arnold Hauser, *The Social History of Art,* (New York: Vintage Books, 1951, Volumes I-IV) Volume 4, pp. 246-249.

budget. They absorb a small slice of expenses compared to what is spent for writers, producers, directors, cameramen, makeup men, art directors, and other technicians. Of course, the more important music is to a film—in publicizing and promoting the feature, in the making of phonograph records—the more crucial their role becomes. This is particularly true for the composer of the score. The better his bargaining position within the production staffs and the bigger his reputation in the studio scene, the more flexibility he will have to write what he wants. More importantly, from the viewpoint of the performers, the more in demand a composer is, the more he can command in salary and number of musicians. Budgets vary with the personal tastes of the producer, writer, director, and other staff, as well as with the style of the production: western, comedy, farce, murder-mystery, fantasy-musical, psychological mystery, romance, social problem, war, horror, etc. Cost structures are closely bound to the scale of production as well as the style: budgets can vary from $10,000 to millions of dollars depending upon the medium, the goals of the studio, and various economic contingencies. All of these factors affect the type of composer hired, the music composed and arranged, and the number of performers hired, as well as the time and care put into the recording of the music.

After the shooting script is filmed and the numerous takes are edited under the director's supervision, a rough cut is viewed by the composer and film staff. Because a bad scene can be improved as well as a good scene ruined, the sequence scores are carefully defined: in style, in the amount and kind of information they can supply about characters, places, "atmosphere," and in building, supporting, and fading scenes. Various suggestions and ideas are discussed and incorporated into the composer's working notes. He then starts to work on the auditory scenarios.

Not only must the score be *compatible* with the screen action, it must be *precisely synchronized* with it. Dramatic time and musical time must fit one another on the reel footage in length so that screen editing and film composition match. Some fundamental problems for the composer (and, at a later stage, the performer) stem from the timing, rhythmic, and pacing contingencies. The film is composed of two distinct parts: the picture image and the sound track. The film reel moves through the camera, and projector, at regular intervals per second. These frames or photographs produce the illusion of continuity when projected on a screen at a rate of 16 or more frames per second. The machinery of 35 mm. film making runs at 24 frames per second. What Arnold Hauser has noted about the distinctive features of film and film making stands equally true for composers and performers.

> The machine is its origin, its medium. . . . Films are "fabricated" and they remain tied to an apparatus, to a machine in a narrower sense than the products of other arts. The machine here stands both between the creative subject and his work and between the receptive subject and his enjoyment of art.[3]

In the division of labor, the technological tie to the film reel imposes a set of constraints which composers and players, as well as their studio counterparts — film editors and sound men — are forced to wrestle with and handle as efficiently as possible. After the working session, a film "breakdown" is furnished the composer by the supervising music editor and his staff. This is a detailed description of the actual film shots, dialogue, sound effects, scene changes, camera angles, dissolves, wipes, and changes in mood. It specifies almost everything that will be important for the composer when he writes the score. As Hauser suggests, the reel stands between the creative composer and his composition. And the breakdown sets forth in

3. Hauser, *op. cit.*, p. 256.

explicit detail the time and timing signposts for the composer to follow.

Several cues are crucial: (1) the reel footage and length of the film sequences he is to compose within, (2) the time, in tenths of a second, at which film action occurs, and (3) the dialogue and action breakdowns. The piano, screen breakdown, metronome, and stop watch are his basic tools. Shaped by terms other than those of purely musical creativity, the composition proceeds on two levels: in the foreground, the thematic material, harmony, orchestration, instrumental texture, and stylistic idiom; underneath, the rhythmic underpinnings. Musical rhythm, pace, and time must be given explicit scrutiny so as to complement and augment the dramatic scene.

Let us take a look at an example of a technique used to synchronize film and music. A screen episode has been selected for scoring, and the breakdown is passed along to the composer by the editors. This particular sequence, let us say, is a chase scene and the film sequence is exactly 60 seconds. The composer decides he will use brass and woodwinds, with a strong driving rhythm in the basses. Thirty bars of music at two bars a second will exactly fit the sequence. He wants a tempo to convey, even to push, the excitement on the screen. He sets the metronome at 120, or 120 quarter notes per minute. In 4/4 time (4 beats per measure, a quarter note receiving one beat), this would then equal 2 beats per second, or 4 beats every two seconds. This would give him a tempo to work with. This technical necessity still leaves much room for personal style, elegance, and plasticity, for within this 60 second, 4/4 pace, he can compose notes with varying rhythmic values (quarter notes, sixteenth notes, etc.). Without getting overly technical, the reel moves at 24 frames per second, so in this episode 48 frames pass through the projector for each 4/4 bar of music. Thus, bars of music and film footage can be matched precisely; this process becomes important when visual cues are imprinted onto the reel for the composer-conductor to follow when directing the studio orchestra. Naturally, the whole act of composition and synchronization becomes very complex when rhythm shifts within a film sequence, when multiple tempi are used during a film segment, and when the thematic line is more complicated.

This set of procedures for film synchronization, however, is only the beginning. Several additional technical operations are performed by the music editor and staff, who further coordinate film and film score. They work out an even more elaborate timetable for the composer's music segments, film breakdowns, and footage. Their jobs are to mark out and then imprint on the reel timing markers or visual cues for the conductor to follow. When the time for studio recording comes, he directs not only from the score (as an orchestra conductor does), but he must also follow the film reel projected before him. The markers can be placed, of course, with a great deal of accuracy given the 24 frames per second. Each frame, for example, has four square holes that fit into the sprockets (or teeth) of the wheel rims on the camera and projection apparatus. With the aid of a small projection machine (movieola) which can be run at various speeds and stopped at any time, a total layout of the reel is possible; reel time and measures of music (even beats per second) are calculated. At this stage, nothing is left to chance. Depending upon how skilled the conductor of the score is, and how technically difficult the writing, the editors imprint visual markers onto the reel. When shown through the projector on the sound recording stage, they are timing signposts and cues. They are the visual counterpart of the metronome. What the composer has written to stop watch and metronome (to serial time and musical time), the editing department further synchronizes with the film celluloid (filming time and actual footage). They prepare those frames which are crucial for the conductor to attend to, such as the following: (1) preparatory measures and rhythm so the conductor and orchestra will know the metronomic pacing of the music, (2) downbeats of measures once the music has started so that the pace will not speed ahead of or fall behind the desired timings, (3) downbeats for particularly crucial sequences of music and film action so that the conductor can anticipate and know exactly where dynamics, phrasing, and motifs appear *in the score* and *on the screen,* and (4) cues for the end of a recording take so that the conductor can see the fades and cutting on the film and coordinate the musicians' performance to them.

Several techniques are used to achieve synchronization. One is the use of "streamers." Following the composer's metronome markings, music editors determine which frames begin right on the metric beats of the measure. A white vertical band is then imprinted onto the frame where the beat occurs and then onto several alternate frames down the footage. When run through the projector on the recording sound stage, they will brightly flash on the large projection screen in back of the orchestra, producing, by persistence of vision, a solid white band. Thus, if the music is written in 4/4, a streamer will appear on the beat of each quarter note. They will move from left to right across the screen, the downbeat of the measure (beat one) at the left and the last beat (beat four) on the right. The last streamer (four) will disappear when it hits the right side of the screen. The next measure or bar of music then begins at the left side of the screen. Like a visual metronome, the bands flash the precise timing onto the screen. Editors can imprint various cues on the reel such as these flashing, metronomic markings, solid bands, or flashing dots. Usually streamers are employed to set the rhythm of the music or to signal the end of a sequence. Dots are used by some studios to spell out; visually, the downbeat of every two or three measures, giving the conductor another set of cues to insure synchronization. He follows both the orchestra score before him and the visual cues. Music editors set these markings onto the celluloid reel and note them on the conductor's score to facilitate his job of uniting the score, and the performance of his musicians.

A third technique is aural rather than visual. It is used in conjunction with these other sets of cues, and here the performing musician is directly involved. Electrical impulses or "clicks" are transmitted to earphones worn by those musicians with the most exposed and rhythmically important instrumental parts. Music editors have imprinted these impulses onto the reel sound track after determining the precise tempi at which the score must be played to match the frames. As a metronome, a hard, metallic syncopation accents metric time. Performance under these conditions depends on considerable high-voltage virtuosity from the musician. The musician must practically sightread his part, closely follow the conductor, listen to the intonation and phrasing of his colleagues, and put this all together with the implacable track pulsations clicking away in his ear. Situations, of course, are complicated when rhythmic events and tempi become more adventurous in chase scenes, animated cartoons, the slick "jingles" which back up TV commercials, and other technically difficult parts. Cartoons are particularly troublesome because of the quick shifts between fast and slow tempi, the former turning the player into a kind of musical speedometer—executing many notes within a short period of time. Problems arise, for example, when the conductor falls behind or directs ahead of the screen cues and click track. Here the musicians are obliged to follow two conflicting sources of time, an impossible task. Musicians, too, can also drag and rush and create problems for the conductor. In order to pull the performers together, the conductor has to unite the two rhythmic grooves. All the performing musicians are expected to face recording problems with nerve, technical brilliance, flexibility, and even cold contempt for these contingencies.

The clicks and visual cues are the recording-studio equivalent of items on a conveyor belt. The belt mechanism is the film reel. Both dramatize the mechanical and automatic nature of moving film and the "laying in" of a composition onto its sound track.

The plan of film assembly, predetermined pacing, and the timing of music in the hands of composers and music editors mean that judgments concerning timing are built into the film process. They are structured by the automatically moving nature of the film and sound synchronization. Performing musicians cannot determine these work techniques or the level at which these "mechanical work rhythms" are employed. They are predetermined at an earlier stage of production before performers are hired to play the film reel scores. A sophisticated recording apparatus accentuates the technological setting and production rationale. Total capital investment in equipment is considerably higher than investment in performing musicians. And at each stage, studio technicians are interposed between the creative and performing musician; the recording stage, which is next in this work process, mirrors the procedures which have preceded it.

The recording sound stage is located in one of the many imposing, windowless structures which dominate the motion picture and television studio lot. In size, sound stages are between middle-sized gymnasiums and airport hangars. Crammed with sets, scaffolding, cables, cameras, microphones, and lighting equipment, they are the major center of production activity when the shooting of a film takes place in the studio and not on location. The major personnel at this stage are the director, art director, cameraman, and sound engineer. Mechanics, carpenters, dollygrips, lamp operators, sound men, wardrobe staff, and actors and actresses perform their technical jobs or fragments of dramatic acting in carrying out the design of the shooting script. Typically, a whole day's shooting will occupy the final edited film for only a few minutes, sometimes a few seconds.

On the recording sound stage, the studio orchestra hired by the contractor is arranged into several major groupings of performers which resemble the physical set-up of a symphony: the *string* sections composed of violin, viola, cello, and bass players; the *woodwind* and *reed* ensemble made up of flute, clarinet, oboe, bassoon, and saxophone instrumentalists; the *brass* ensemble of trumpet, trombone, tuba, and French horn players; and the *percussion* section of several musicians playing a wide variety of instruments such as timpani, snare drums, vibraphone, cymbals, etc. One or two pianists, harpists, and guitarists round out this large studio orchestra. Above the musicians, microphones of different sizes dangle securely from wires connected to the tips of long mike booms, or fishpoles. These "booms" extend their arms over the orchestra at various angles and heights, and microphone cables and a complex array of adjustment wires travel along their arms, which are anchored to tall frameworks stationed around the orchestra. On the floor, recording cables and earphone cords run between the performers' music stands and chairs.

The podium faces these players, and the conductor looks out over this maze of sound equipment to the film screen which is in back of the players and dominates the

stage setting. Above and behind the podium are the projection and recording booths. The sound engineers are
responsible for the quality of orchestral sound, balance,
volume, and sonority; they make sure that the stage microphones are set up correctly, so that the instrumental
texture and blend is clear and that harmonic distortions
and unwanted resonances are minimized. The engineers
sit in front of an elaborate console by which they control
the mike input onto the recording tape tracks. The projectionists are in charge of setting up the film segments and
rewinding them as the recording takes are rehearsed and
performed in synchronization with the reels. Thus, the
sound engineers handle the recording of the orchestra
onto tape, the projectionists handle the film reels, and the
music editor coordinates the sound and film.

Recording the sound for the film sequences is done in
the following way: after the score is written and further
edited in time and timing cues by the music staff, the parts
are orchestrated and arranged, and a team of music copyists go to work. The performers are hired by the contractor, typically for a three-hour call. The conductor
gives the musicians a few instructions about the style,
timing, emphasis, and, when appropriate, the solo parts
for a particular musical sequence. They run through the
music once or twice to check these and also to spot
copying errors. When the soundmen are satisfied with the
balance they are getting through the microphones, and
when mikes and their sound levels are adjusted, a rehearsal with the click tracks and visual cues can begin. The
projectionist starts the film reel, the edited streamers start
across the screen, and the orchestra prepares for the conductor's downbeat. The music starts and is performed
continuously through the sequence unless audible mistakes in notes or rhythm occur. After this rehearsal, a recording take begins. The studio bell rings, a red light above the

screen goes on, the projectionist starts the reel, the sound-men turn on the multi-track tape recorders, and the streamers, dots, and clicks begin. Usually the same music sequence is recorded several times in succession; after the takes or at the end of several takes, the players and staff will listen to their performance (the playback) on the huge speakers around the sound stage. When several satisfactory takes have been made on one section, the rehearsal of another begins. The musicians turn to the next piece of music, the projectionist sets up the film reel, and the soundmen prepare another tape on their machines.

The time allotted for recording varies with the complexity of the score, the length of the music, and the size of the film budget. Unavoidable problems can occur from take to take: the conductor misses a cue; he moves out of "sync" with the screen action; somebody misses a note, spoiling the recording and making it necessary to stop the orchestra, rewind the film reels and tape, and start again; the balance for one take is not correct for another one; the soloist misses some notes he has played perfectly two times before. The studio pro's job is to handle these pressures as efficiently as possible. He is part of the technical and organizational setting where mistakes are costly and where one's performance batting average must be consistently high.

Despite the low overall budget expenditure for music and musicians, studio recording is seen as an expensive operation. The wage scales are set for recording musicians in motion picture and television film on the basis of a three-hour session and on the size of the orchestra; the fewer musicians, the higher the scale. For television film, the Federation has set a basic minimum of scoring hours (the amount and length of live music) for two types of productions: dramatic and non-dramatic. For 13 half-hour episodes of a dramatic show, for example, 21 scoring hours of live music are necessary to meet the union regulations. For non-dramatic productions, 18 scoring hours (or 6 three-hour calls for those players who are hired) are necessary. In 1970, theatrical motion pictures with a budget of $350,000 or more, using 35 or more musicians, have a basic scale of $75.58 per musician, with the leader receiving double this amount. Commercial jingles are particularly lucrative; basic scale for a one-hour call using 5 or more musicians is $40.

When the director or conductor is satisfied with the performance the soundmen have on tape, the recording session is complete. Next the composer-conductor and the music film editor decide which are the best takes. And the last stage of post-production is synchronizing and dubbing the music with the action of the film; four sets of reels must be put together: music reel, picture reel, and sound effects reel. At the dubbing stage, music, sound effects, and dialogue are "laid onto" one single reel of magnetic film. The music film editor fits the music onto these magnetic transfers so the picture reel and the music match exactly. This, incidentally, is the same process whereby pre-recorded music (or "track" when reused from a previous TV segment) is put on the sound reel. In my example, however, the music is original and the time and reel length are synchronized. With "canned music" the score is not written for the specific scene; it is not timed precisely and must be shortened, lengthened, and edited to fit the film reel. When these procedures are completed by the music film cutters and editors, we have the composite track. When it is assembled, it is played back through speakers, and if the production staff find the sound recording, "mixing," and synchronization satisfactory, it is re-recorded onto a negative film and developed. The negative film picture track and sound track are combined. They produce the positive print, the finished product. When the positive is run through the projection apparatus, the lens projects 24 picture frames per second onto the screen and the sound head puts dialogue, music, sound effects, etc. through an amplifier into the speakers.

If musicians want to see their contribution to the total film, they have to go to the motion picture theater, watch the television program on their sets or, in the case of records, get a copy of the recording. How the orchestra will eventually sound on the finished track, after the final mixing and dubbing, is determined by other technicians. This is true for other studio work such as the backings for rock groups, singers, TV commercials, and "live" TV variety programs. These are all part of the intimately subdivided nature of sound and film *production,* and their electronic *reproduction.* In describing the perspectives of free-lance musicians, we must understand the nature of this work environment in which problems arise in spite of these performers' efforts to control them: the lone free-lancer has little control over poor studio administrative practices and marketing conditions, work scheduling, inadequate rehearsal time, unchallenging music, mediocre conducting, fads and fashions in the film business, techniques of recording, inferior recording equipment, or the final disposition of his musical efforts.

Free-Lancers and the Hiring Structure

In the commercial music business, the term free-lance has two related meanings. It refers to a type of hiring practice typically employed on a wage, or job-by-job, basis, and it designates an area of work performed by those bearing the name. Free-lance musicians are hired on a short-term basis: contracts between an employer and a musician cover only the work at hand; they terminate when the job is completed and the musician is paid. Thus, unlike symphony orchestra musicians, or those who hold staff positions in radio and television stations and legitimate theaters, or other musicians on long-term contracts, the free-lance musician is not contractually affiliated with any one organization or commercial enterprise. Like other free-lancers (writers, photographers, detectives), he competes for jobs in a market where his ability, reputation, tact, and social contacts determine the nature and volume of his work. He is a musical entrepreneur — a musician for hire.

To the outsider, this hiring practice seems hopelessly fragmented and unorganized. But, while it underscores the predominantly casual nature of studio employment within the film and music settings, it also sets up social conditions for informal orbits of power, privilege, and prestige. These orbits shape the work and careers of commercial musicians in Los Angeles.

"On call" refers to hiring agreements and practices which take place between orchestra contractors and free-lance performers. The music contractor is the person in charge of hiring musicians for a studio's productions. After a production is scored by the composer, the music contractor must be familiar with the talent available, know the individual skills of the musicians, understand the needs and desires of the composer and conductor, and, on the basis of his experience and bargaining power, hire the best musicians he can. The music contractor is in charge of putting together the best available orchestra; the music department of the film and recording studio rely on him to hire the most proficient and efficient performers available.

On the free-lance stock exchange, the market value of some players is of considerable magnitude; through this system of preference, these performers who are in great demand for studio work constitute an inner circle. While there is considerable intrigue and competition for studio jobs, this term in no way connotes a conspiracy of some against others. It means a loosely organized group of colleagues having common characteristics, namely, their demand position and volume of work, which separate them from others on the musical scene. (See Appendix A for a more extensive treatment.) This occupational situation represents a stratification of studio work, and it is a means of organizing the free-lance labor market.

Musicians who are on call and called by the studios occupy a privileged position on a contractor's list of preferred musicians. The higher the musician is on the list, the more calls he gets and work he does. The more lists a musician is on, the more chances he has of being called. Below these free-lancers are the musicians who fill out the work call; they comprise the rest of the orchestra. Still very much in demand for studio work, they are hired after the inner orbit, the "cream of the crop."

These overlapping circles of players do all the film and recording dates in Los Angeles. Around them are musicians at various stages of their careers: some who have lost their market value or popularity, and others who are doing casual work in local orchestras, big bands, rehearsal groups, nightclub gigs, and dances.

Becker and Strauss state that, "Institutions, at any given moment, contain people at different stages in their careers. Movement and changes at each level are in various ways dependent on those occurring at other levels. One way of uncovering the interdependence of careers is to ask: Who are the important *others* at various stages of their career. . . ?"[4] No matter what stage a free-lancer has reached, his career is interdependent on his colleagues'

4. Howard S. Becker and Anselm L. Strauss, "Careers, Personality and Adult Socialization," *American Journal of Sociology* LXII (November, 1959), pp. 261–262.

careers, as well as on what is happening to contractors, composers, and arrangers.

One can identify crucial points in a career, the speed of advancement, and the timetable of achievement by knowing how often and by which studios a musician is called. Seen from the inside, the jurisprudence of studio calls is a persistent occupational problem. The culture of free-lance work contains conventional understandings about the musician and others: why some work more than others, why some get work and lose it, which contractors are loyal and which are disagreeable SOB's, and which musicians are cut-throats or not aggressive enough. Members' problems vary with position. Considerable strain, intrigue, and style arise from the efforts of studio players to maintain some sustained control over their chances in the hiring-power game between contractor, studio, and musician.

At the top of free-lance work are the players who work in the motion picture, television film, and recording studios. These musicians are chosen by contractors, leaders, and composers; some are more in demand than others. Those most in demand have access to the best paying, and often most musically interesting, types of work. When a contractor puts together an orchestra, these musicians are the first to be considered. There are 15 to 20 major contractors who allocate the work in the studio, and the same group of popular musicians are chosen for the "best studio work" in Los Angeles. Therefore contractors are in competition for the services of these musicians.

Some film studios have what is termed a first-call policy in which musicians informally assure the contractor that they will take calls as long as they are notified 96 hours before the work date begins. After that time, the musician is free to accept other calls. In exchange, the free-lancer receives some loyalty from the film studio. He will work when the production scores call for his instrument. This formal system within the informal free-lance structure is left over from the days of the contract studio orchestra, when the major studios had a stable orchestra of musicians. With the end of the contracts in the late fifties, some studios retained their instrumentalists by means of first-call policy. Those film enterprises with more productions and more work for musicians were, of course, in a better position to establish and sustain the 96-hour agreement, for they could offer the free-lance player some stability of work within a predominantly casual hiring market.

Since this changeover to the new non-contractual system, the overall employment situation for the musician has changed radically. Despite the desire of some film studios to maintain their musicians, composers and conductors can request that the contractor hire those they feel most comfortable with in the recording situation. First-call musicians are subject to change in orchestra size as instrumental sections are reduced, and are generally more susceptible to the vagaries of the film industry than they were while under contract.

Within the casual employment structure of the film industry, composers and conductors hired to do a film score frequently have preferences in their choice of musicians. Through their work in the industry, they come to feel more confident conducting particular players. Composers often write instrumental parts with particular musicians in mind and simply like the sound, efficiency, and personality of certain instrumentalists. Unlike the contract studio orchestras, the present free-lance orchestras within the industry are subject to personnel changes, when, for example, different composers and conductors desire "their" musicians over the studio's players. Thus a musician on call at one studio can be hired to play at another if requested by the composer-conductor, whereas under the

contract orchestra system, union regulations and quota
restrictions constrained musicians to work in their home
studio. Today, under the free-lance system, a musician
theoretically can work at all the studios, depending upon
his reputation and availability.

The status structure of the orchestra itself is related to
the choices of composers, conductors, and contractors.
Specifically, recurring patterns of tension and problems
are generated by one's position in an orchestra; where one
sits closely matches where one stands socially. The terms
"first chair," "second chair," "section man," "first chair
soloist," or the more familiar "concertmaster" reflect the
prestige given to which part one plays. Presumably the
better or more important (more exposed) the part, the
more competent and important the player. The contractor
has an interest in hiring those whom he recognizes as the
best players; at the top of his list are those who can play
principal parts. These typically are the preferred studio
pros. In hiring, then, he starts with those he evaluates as
"most desirable" and moves down the list to the players
who will fill out the instrumental section. When the violin
section is hired, he begins with the concertmaster, then
second chair, and down the list. He might even ask the
concertmaster which musicians he would prefer. Naturally, in this status game of musical chairs, some can acquire
reputations as top players or section men; the former will
be more in demand by the majority of studios and contractors. They are the pros who are cool and poised under
pressure and who can play any part under any condition
and are of proven worth; they make few mistakes. That
other performers on the list are of equal ability, perhaps
even of superior talent, is not crucial to the contractor.
His job is made easier, and more efficient, by the weight
of precedent and thus he turns automatically to the stable
studio men; those who make up the inner circle.

The musicians' careers and the contractors' careers are interdependent. This inter-dependence works both ways, for if musicians are subject to the social preferences of contractors, the contractor is also subject to the evaluation of those who depend on his talents. His position of prestige and authority rests on the quality of musical organizations he assembles, the quality of solo men, a smoothly running hiring setup, and his ability to please the composer who has written the music and the conductor who must direct the studio performance of it. His job is full of tension and intrigue. Success in the studios depends on his ability to coordinate the schedules of a group of highly talented, sensitive, and busy musical entrepreneurs. He uses a wide spectrum of techniques to get the musicians he wants in the orchestra. Exchange is the basic ingredient. By offering assurances of future calls, by cashing in on past alliances, and by the use of tactful negotiation with other contractors, he exchanges high paying studio work for loyalty. The more loyalty, the more likely the free-lancer will be near the top of the list. He is jealous of his prerogatives and protective of the musicians in "his stable"; and the promises and threats which are part of this exchange relationship can assure or irritate musicians. They also reveal the vulnerability of both parties to excessive demands — demands which are part of the delicate balance in *quid pro quo* practices of free-lance work.

The role of the musicians' union exacerbates these problems. Wage scales and working conditions for the motion picture and television film studios are set by negotiated, collective bargaining agreements between the studios and the American Federal of Musicians, Local 47. They do not, however, contain any stipulations about the minimum number of musicians to be used on production calls, nor can the union demand that a studio or contractor hire a particular number of musicians, or censure employers for any unjust hiring or firing episodes. Unlike other craft unions, the musicians' union has little control over the labor market, offers no apprenticeship program, and, since the days of the contract orchestras, provides only wage scales, rest periods, minimum scoring hours and amount of music per TV series. Control over job rights is negligible. Career fates, then, are dependent on sponsorship, loyalty, and reputation; colleagues, contractors, composers, and conductors shape the individual career movement and, thereby, the larger studio scene.

CHAPTER THREE

Career Problems, Comparative Failure, and Going Commercial

Career decisions are perhaps among the most problematic and fateful for members in our society. As individuals pursue their careers within the framework of a given setting or by moving from one setting to another, there are certain turning points or climactic periods which are more threatening than others. How a person deals with these conditions is an important determinant of his fate. The materials that follow analyze the meaning of studio musicians' career moves into commercial work, or the decision to go commercial. They are all derived from the respondents' occupational histories and open-ended questions concerning their aspirations and reasons for starting a career in commercial work.

The most striking features of these performers' views of their career lines and aspirations are the heightened affect and sheer saliency of these issues. Undoubtedly, the ego involvement which comes into play when asking respondents to give retrospective accounts of their past contributed to the long, elaborate, and at times, emotional nature

51

of responses. It became clear very early in the research that the meaning of a career to the respondent is evaluated differently depending on how the objective features of the career matched the member's subjective ideal aspirations. Musicians differ by type of instrument and by their ambitions, role models, ideals, career problems, and personal adjustments.

The working question for this chapter is the following: What are the structural conditions which account for the positive and negative meanings attached to career moves into commercial work? Comparisons between different kinds of performers lead to a description and analysis of three substantive areas: First, the idea of comparative failure among musicians developed; second, a discussion of the conditions under which the sense of failure is or is not intensified; third, the foregoing were compared with Becker's observations concerning dance band musicians and their responses to going commercial; and, finally, consideration was given to some of the implications of these ideas. Hopefully, this research will lead to greater understanding of a career in the music business which should help both younger musicians in making their decision more wisely and possibly those who have already made these decisions to place their experiences in a broader context.

Comparative Failure and Scaling Down Aspirations

The concept of comparative failure has been used to describe the fact that people engaged in consistent lines of activity (1) designate a certain group to serve as a point of reference, (2) which they use to make judgments about the attributes or values which they themselves possess (status, success, the self), and that (3) when they compare themselves to these reference points, they perceive themselves as having failed. It is an evaluation resulting from social comparison; estimates of attributes or values vary according to the reference group.

Comparative failure is built into many occupations and careers. Recognition and fame are strongly emphasized in the artistic as well as in the scientific community. Both fields are populated by great men to whom one compares one's achievement and against whom one is likely to fail.[1] A persistent career problem for some of the studio musicians is their feeling of comparative failure as solo artists. They failed as concert performers. Three conditions intensify this trend: first, for many violin, cello, and viola players, the seeds of professional aspiration to be a concert artist and soloist have been planted in their lives before their teens.[2] Solo repertoire is learned and constantly perfected during these and subsequent years of intensive training. The performer becomes, in fact, a small-scale virtuoso. Second, achievement of fame as a concert artist is strongly stressed by those responsible for the cultivation of values, outlook, and abilities. Recognition for brilliance in the solo role is heavily emphasized by music teachers, friends, fellow colleagues, and most often, a determined family. Competition and public performance sharpen the edges of ambition. Third, the musician exists in a society where the concert stage, phonograph record-

1. Barney G. Glaser, *Organizational Scientists: Their Professional Careers* (Indianapolis: The Bobbs-Merrill Company, Inc., 1964), pp. 129-136.

2. Seventy-five per cent of the free-lancers interviewed began playing a musical instrument before they were 12 years old; a majority of string performers began their present instrument before they were 8 years old; woodwind, reed, brass, and percussion performers report they began playing their instrument between the ages 9 and 13. Unlike other occupations, the decision to earn a living in music was made very early in life, in the majority of cases before the respondent was 18 years old. Moreover, most of these musicians were in fact making a solid living for themselves before they were 20.

ings, television, and music schools constantly and loudly proclaim the glory and highlight the visibility of the string virtuoso. Heifetz, Stern, Menuhin, Piatigorsky and other great artists become role models, the points of reference on which career horizons are erected. They become the standards by which personal success in music is evaluated. Eiduson's observations concerning scientists are appropriate in discussing the dynamics of ideal comparisons. The aspiring scientist, she says, ". . . lift[s] his gods to Olympian slopes. The model, then, is the ego ideal figure, who represents the ultimate position and, in fact, defines what a scientist should do, how he should think, how he should act."[3] Judging the pace and terrain of his own career climb in a solo musical career or in the scientific elite, the actor has not risen fast enough (or even gained a foothold) on these exalted slopes. Comparing himself against the masters, he may come to see himself of lesser stature for not having achieved the recognition or even the high-level virtuosity and elegance of the great charismatic figures of the past and present.

The cognitive contours of comparative failure emerged in interviews with studio violinists and cellists. A large proportion of these respondents reported that during their early years, before their teens, they aspired to be concert soloists. Only a handful, however, actually accomplished this goal; some only saw the faint beginnings of the ideal career line. Almost all were eloquent in relating their early careers as child protegés, giving accounts replete with anecdotes of their famous teachers, and outlining the beginnings of their lives as potential soloists. To give the reader a good idea of the content and language of these personal horizons, a few excerpts from interviews with

3. Bernice T. Eiduson, *Scientists: Their Psychological World* (New York: Basic Books, 1962), pp. 189–190.

musicians who started their careers as soloists are presented. In these cases a similar retrospective tale of difficulty is told, accounts of career moves are threaded with attempts to bridge the fracture between dreams and deeds. The similarity of vocabularies for justifying moves away from the solo ideal was striking.

The first respondent is a violinist who started playing very early in life. By his teens he had begun a concert tour but, because of the Depression, moved into commercial radio in the East, and then into the Hollywood studios during the 1940's. The Depression, the disproportion of successful to unsuccessful solo artists, and family responsibilities are the themes that appear in a number of musicians' reflections about their career histories.

> The Depression put an end to my concert hopes, but I earned a living right through it while others were out of work; the music business was good during that period and it paid real well. The way I look at it, a fellow gets to be 25 and is capable, and can play his instrument, and has worked hard, and has the potential of a fine artist, but he gets married and has to make a living, so he starts playing commercially, and there you are. . . . How many concert artists can this society afford? A handful, that's all. You can count them . . . Heifetz, Menuhin, Stern, Rose . . . a handful, and this during your lifetime and mine.

The next respondent takes up a similar theme, but goes a step further is pulling together the fabric of aspirations and the problems of a solo career.

> Q: During these early years you were a soloist?
> Yes. I left school early and studied privately, playing concerts, touring — the whole life of an artist. The trouble is I had to make a living, and you can't do that concertizing. The expense of everything is enormous. It's *impossible* to survive on a concert career. I suppose commercial work . . . well . . .
> Q: Did you want to do it, did you regard it as temporary or what?

Hell no. I've *never* wanted to do it, but I wasn't actually ambitious enough to try to change it. You see it's primarily again a question of economics. I mean one can be very idealistic and ambitious, but if you want to raise a family and put your children through college . . . unless, you're so driven with ambition that everything else falls by the way-side . . . well, you simply must sublimate everything to your career and then you might make it; but even *then* it's rough.

An older violinist, who was unusually articulate, gave the following account of his early career:

I started studying when I was about six years old. It was foisted upon me by my parents. It became part of my life and I sort of grew up with it feeling it was a necessity. Then when I was about twelve years old, that time I studied with one of the finest teachers in the world. Then I began to attend concerts, and listen to these great violinists; it became part of an inspiration to go on with it. Then the study, tours, and Europe; to play was part of a pattern. I gave my American debut and then an impresario lined up concerts throughout the United States.

Q: What years were these?

. . . That was the extent, it may be regrettable or not, as time will bear out, of the concert phase of my career. The reason for the brevity was the fact that the manager, the concert manager I had at that time, and he was certainly no different from any other manager then or even in this day, they could only do so much for an artist in presenting him. And then in order to exploit him or her, there would have to be, well, at that time, [there was] a set amount of money for the promotion of the artist, like selling a new automobile tire or something. And that far back a certain amount of money would take an artist a long way. . . . Today, of course, you have to have a fortune to launch anyone on a big career because it's a peculiarity, especially of the American people, the enormous amount of advertising, the amount of promotion that goes on in this country. One may be a fine artist, performer, dancer, singer or anything, but they must have a certain amount of promotion behind them in order for the public to be name-conscious of them and interested in them and hearing about this or that person, to go to hear them play or see them play or whatever. And unless that is possible, the artist will only have a difficult time making himself known. So at that particular time the funds were not available, so my father felt that he had already put enough thousands of dollars into my study career that he just didn't have to go on with it. And that was the end of the concert career.

Q: What happened then?

I felt qualified to try a different area in the musical field in order to earn a good living. I know some of my contemporaries have fallen by the wayside and did not, or could not, adapt themselves to another field of music, like commercial music. I felt that every phase had its importance in life. I've actually done very well for myself, I'm very busy and I like to work.

Presumably the allusion is to his contemporaries who were reluctant to scale down their solo career aspirations and move into the commercial field. The above material is indicative of the eminently practical language that appears over and over again while these respondents discuss their careers. Pride in their personal ability to adjust and the satisfaction of working hard, earning a good living, supporting a family, and "being realistic" comprise the outstanding features of this outlook. In the interviews with string players, there were numerous anecdotes about "facing reality" and, conversely, the pitfalls of "ivory tower idealism." The correspondence between past aspirations and career line is all the more apparent in some of the thoughtful reflections given by these string players. Along with expressions of being "realistic" were frequent statements about the fate of personal idealism: "Ideals are fine when you're young, but you got to earn a living and as you grow older you find they just don't work out and that's it."

Here is one of the older string players who stressed not a few times the meaning of being realistic. The following is in response to a question asked of each respondent.

Q: Early in your life, what ideally did you want to be if everything went your way?

Well, that's another thing . . . early in my life I was very fortunate to have a teacher who was very realistic and I've tried to carry out his philosophy. I think the biggest mistake is that everyone is trained to be a great soloist. I know my colleagues in the studios are all disappointed, they're making money but they didn't quite make it musically, they didn't make it as soloists. You have to be very realistic about it, there's only room for seven or eight soloists in this world. And you've got to think of the economic side of it too. A real musician sort of lives a Jekyll and Hyde existence, playing the kind of music you love, string quartets, sonatas, and then the other side of it, the commercial, which makes it all possible. You want to get married, buy a house, buy a fiddle, and it all takes money. I would say I was flexible. I'm a realist, unlike some of my colleagues.

The above material is indicative of the correspondence between lowering personal ideals or "cooling down" career aspirations and the shift to new judgments for comparing individual career success. Almost all of the violin and cello players, and to a lesser extent viola players, emphasized that they aspired to be soloists. Their adjustments to perceived comparative failure involve several related lines of adaptation.

First, their accounts verbally suppress or render less memorable their earlier, and higher, horizons. The most obvious mechanism is to turn away from the unattainable towards new, if lesser, career terrain; they cultivated other options and made themselves available for new points of reference. Frank, if not cynical, expressions are given about the ways in which they became, or were forced to become, more "realistic."

Second, the bitterness expressed at becoming "realistic" is directed at forces which impede success as an artist rather than at the ideals themselves and their concrete embodiment in the great charismatic heroes of the concert stage. In this way, these players salvage ideals strained by the reality of their actual careers and provide for themselves an acceptable vocabulary for explaining their moves into commercial work. Their language emphasizes prosaic contingencies. Economic pressures, marriage, promotion problems, the Depression, and high proportion of unsuccessful to successful soloists are all dominant in a perspective that might be labeled realistic apologia. Like the aspiring jazz musicians Becker worked with and talked to, these once-aspiring soloists harbor less than favorable views about the business of music, promoters, and the "ignorant" consuming public.

Third, an intriguing justification affirms both the value of "cooling down" and commercial success. After comparing himself with his string-playing colleagues, the respondent agrees that they, like himself, did indeed fail to achieve the fame and glory of a concert career. Self evaluation is obviously in terms of peers, not "stars." As peers, they are all in the same boat; however, in contrast to his colleagues, our respondent says that he is different. While agreeing that most violin, cello, and viola players are disappointed, even disillusioned with the music business, the respondent has been flexible. He has adapted by making a "realistic" and smoother adjustment, by facing these crucial career contingencies squarely while others have not. Moreover, he implies that his adaptation is the kind others ought to make when they "go commercial." He points out that he moved faster than these other "idealists" towards economic success. In leaving these comparative-reference individuals behind, he views himself as better than they. Thus, "cooling down" becomes a virtuous process in itself. The career decision to move into studio work, and its greener pastures, is seen as a success.

Those on the fringes of or outside the high-paying inner circle of Hollywood studio work cannot so easily rely on the rationale of being realistic. They have trouble intoning the success theme. They are comparative failures in a double sense. First, in terms of the ideal solo models, they have clearly not "made it." And second, in terms of movement up the more prosaic, but nevertheless competitive, rungs of the commercial ladder they have failed to climb as fast or as high as their colleagues. To speculate somewhat, for violinists more than cellists or violists there is a greater likelihood of comparative failure with respect to the illustrious role models despite an objectively satisfactory career climb in the studios. More than others, these respondents have a residue of failure independent of their position in the studio scene. Probably the reason for this difference lies in the more visible portrait of the solo violinist as the virtuoso or concert "star" *par excellence* (next to pianists).

And finally, because studio work gives the successful inner-circle performer a life-style and freedom to pursue his leisure interests, "going commercial" need not necessarily inhibit the attainment of some of his musical ideals. This is the Jekyll-and-Hyde motif mentioned by the older violin player, and it is an outlook that is found with great frequency among many of these performers.

Put simply, studio work serves as a means to the attainment of ends outside itself. The respondent views himself as a comparative success in that he has made it in the studios while salvaging lower, but valued, musical goals. Not a few nurture and actively pursue musical performance for their own satisfaction outside of the studios. The reader will find statements about playing chamber music, concerts, and teaching throughout the illustrative materials which follow. In its most extreme form, some respondents claimed that commercial work is one of the only forms of employment in the country which gives a musician the opportunity to earn a good living for his family and still have the time and energy to "play what he wants." The social backdrop for these statements is very simple. Asked why they moved into studio work, the respondents set the Jekyll-and-Hyde theme against the anonymity, unhappiness, and tension of the symphony orchestra as a career choice and work setting.

Impact of Aspirations on Orchestral Careers

Among former orchestral violin and cello instrumentalists, there were a few supportive comments of the intrinsic or extrinsic — either musical or economic — rewards of his line of activity. A most common outlook is one which evokes a rather grimly remembered time of financial difficulty. In looking back, they reflect on the sharp distinction between past rewards in the orchestra and those now enjoyed in the Hollywood studios.

In terms of ideal aspirations and career goals, their lack of enthusiasm for the orchestra is more provocative. Only a handful report they ideally wanted to be symphony musicians. A sizable number, however, did in fact work in that setting before their twenties. For some of the violin players, it seemed as if there was little distinction to be made between moving to the orchestra and going commercial. Both occasioned some personal turmoil, redefinition of occupational self-image, and, in their words, "becoming realistic." It was clearly a career turning point they grudgingly accepted.[4] Here is a younger violin player who was working in an orchestra before his twenties; he underlines many of the complaints reported by his colleagues during these interviews.

4. These findings support Antek's observations about symphony musicians based on his years in the string section of the NBC Symphony, "... hardly a string player in a major symphony today, with the exception of bass players ... did not aspire to a concert or chamber-music career." *This Was Toscanini* (New York: Vanguard Press, 1963), p. 71.

The symphony never impressed me as a place I wanted to spend the rest of my life in, the anonymity of it all, being brow-beaten by conductors and all that. At seventeen I was able to earn a living. My father didn't like the idea at all; he wanted me to be a concert artist, but you have to be realistic. After I was released from the service, I was in L.A. and so I started to free-lance; the pay was good.

Here is a middle-aged cellist, a warm and friendly man whose anger begins to seep into the conversation when asked about the years spent in two major orchestras. He does not talk about it easily, as his colleague did above. He begins by emphasizing that work in the studios gave him enough money and freedom to do the things he really wanted to do; again, the predominantly utilitarian Jekyll-and-Hyde view of commercial work. He then proceeds to detail his dissatisfaction with the orchestra in general, and one conductor in particular. He and the following respondents are quoted at length because of the serious and sophisticated commentary on their own solutions to the tensions of orchestra work.

The studios allowed me to do other things, chamber music . . . God, day in and day out in an orchestra, you'd get cabin fever with all the pressure . . . and lousy pay on top of it. You have very few personalities conducting today that I would devote my life and energies to. The job, maybe; the conductor, no. There are few who inspire me. Take the conductor of the Y Orchestra. There was no better example of a great conductor and son of a bitch at the same time. In that type of situation, you're torn because you can make marvelous music, precise music, dramatic music — but you don't exactly enjoy the process with a man like that. I feel life is too short, so why grind yourself into a single job that you aren't happy with? I'm lucky to be working in this town, nowhere else can you make such money. It's great if you can crack the business.

The next musician is an older violinist. Loquacious and thoughtful, he was one of the most clearly dissatisfied respondents. At the outset of the interview he went into an illuminating discussion comparing the economic and musical features of symphony work and commercial jobs.

Q: What were some of the steps that lead you into commercial work?

When I got out of the Navy, I decided not to return to the symphony, so I waited around for awhile and I got a job in radio.

Q: That was out here (Los Angeles)?

Yes. And we played, it was a 15-minute show, we did it twice a day. And there were four violins with a jazz band. And all we did actually was to play whole notes, called footballs. We played very little. But we made $226 a week, base. At that time, the symphony was paying $60 or $70 and it occurred to me . . . I said to myself, with all the work of the symphony, and the degree of knowledge that was necessary, and to play that music, any beginner could play the radio show, and get paid three times as much . . . at least. And so it didn't seem right, you know. But anyway, I think that's the motivation for people who are in symphonies, they all want to get into the free-lance field, 'cause that's where all the money is . . . And also the work load . . . you see it's very difficult and you can't get four or five concerts a week for, like, 30 weeks in a row and it's very tough. . . . In this country the ability and training is there, but there's no way of using it. I think that's one of the reasons why today string players are hard to find. All the major symphonies are just looking. They just can't find young people to come into symphonies with the proper training. This business is a jingle. There are only a few string players who really enjoy what they're doing, the rest just struggle in this jingle. The only solution is government subsidy of the arts on a nation-wide scale.

The next respondent is a former orchestra musician, now one of the string players in the inner circle. In discussing his career, he sets forth many of the familiar themes found in the remarks of other musicians quoted above. He emphasizes the importance of supporting a

family, that Los Angeles was a good place to move to, and
that the money in commercial work was exceptional. He
also points to a theme that is implicit in other respondents'
views of the symphony entrapment in a collective setting.
Here are some excerpts from the interview which lasted
more than two and half hours.

Q: You were with the S Orchestra in the forties?

Yes. I started in the last stand of course. Then I was on the
second stand when I quit. And one of the reasons that I quit
is that I used to have a special salary and then they had bad
times there, but later raised the minimum and wouldn't raise
any extra amount. Well, they gave me a hard luck story about
how bad conditions were, so finally I thought I'd better move.
I should have left many years earlier. I thought I was sort of
buried in that town.

Q: What do you mean by that?

There's nothing else in (that city) except the orchestra. I did a
little teaching, but it didn't amount to too much. There was no
opportunity to make much money and the salary of the orchestra was pretty low at that time, and it was quite a hard-
ship to try to raise a family on that salary. New York would
be quite different; they have . . . I mean, a symphony man can
take outside work. Of course there's L.A.

Q: So this is why you came to L.A.?

Yes . . . to raise a family, and it was a better deal all around.
The salary was better and it also gave me a chance to play a
lot of chamber music, concerts, and something that is more
rewarding musically than just commercial work. An orchestra's quite a grind, there's not really a chance to play
—especially for the string player—unless you're a concertmaster . . . you're just a small cog in a big piece of machinery.
And there's no satisfaction other than if you're playing with
one of the world giants, then it's quite an experience, but the
run-of-the-mill conductor doesn't mean anything; in fact, he's
a big bore.

Q: By your twenties you were already in the orchestra setting?

I was either 20 or 21 . . . I always thought of making a living and of course I got married when I was 21 too, so that. . . . I never had a strong desire to push my career farther and farther. I thought I had worked hard in the conservatory and I'd achieved a certain level and that was it. Now the next thing was to try to feed myself and family.

On the basis of these retrospective interpretations of career moves out of the orchestra, several elements of these respondents' outlooks point to the gradual erosion of commitment to this line of activity. Some of these features are linked to the orchestra's career ladder, others to the concrete work situation, and still others to family and life-cycle contingencies. Becker has argued that commitment, in this case to an occupation, occurs when the actor finds he has, deliberately or not, accumulated valuables which he would have to relinquish if he moved to another line of activity.[5] Members often make side bets or stake some originally extraneous interest on pursuing a career. These interests become bound into, and constrain, future activity. The greater the stake and involvement of these side bets in his present occupational and career activity, the greater the commitment. And to turn it about, the fewer valuables accumulated and payoffs acquired, the less the staying power of commitment. If decisions not supported by side bets lack staying power, so do those in which these bets are seen as poor bargains.

Awareness of alternative lines rendered the studio musicians' commitment to the orchestral setting increasingly more shallow and correspondingly heightened

5. Howard S. Becker, "Notes on the Concept of Commitment," *American Journal of Sociology* LXVI (July, 1960), 32–40. For an excellent overview of this issue see Blanche Geer, "Occupational Commitment and the Teaching Profession," in *Institutions and the Persons,* edited by Howard Becker, *et al.* (Chicago: Aldine Publishing Co., 1968), pp. 221-234.

their willingness to risk a move onto another career escalator in the studios. Their outlooks are strikingly similar. There was little to be lost from going commercial. The commercial scene is viewed as having facilitated the acquisition of those valuables so difficult to come by in the symphony: money, opportunity to play chamber music, and leisure. The combination of more successful handling of family and life-cycle contingencies and larger amounts of leisure appear to have resulted in more constraining valuables than any other feature of Hollywood studio work.

Quite apart from the now familiar theme of little economic payoff, few musicians demonstrated any real enthusiasm for autocratic conductors, demanding work schedules, and the uses to which their skills were put in this setting. Their original zest for moving out of the orchestra is easily seen in members' accounts of playing in the string ensemble. To exaggerate the picture somewhat, it seemed as if these ex-symphony musicians failed in their attempts to *not* become orchestral ensemble players. They have staked their pride and self-esteem on their abilities as high powered performers; they have invested a great deal of time and money and a tremendous amount of effort in preparing themselves. In scaling down their aspirations, many have trouble coming to grips with the fact that they are working, in many instances, as ensemble players, not concertmasters or soloists. Many talked about their work in the orchestra as if they were assembly-line workers. The phrase "cogs in a big machine" came up several times, not only to emphasize some of the reasons why they moved out of the orchestra, but also to portray much of their present studio work. Some went so far as to claim that their skills and talents deteriorate in the symphony due to the grind of repetitive work and uninspired performances. While this view may be overdrawn, it nevertheless indicates one major contingency blocking the easy acquisition of work-connected valuables. Theoretically, it points to the importance of what they bring to the orchestral setting in terms of prior commitments;[6] the lack of sufficient constraining valuables found in ensemble work is linked to skills acquired in the past and former mobility aspirations.

The violinists and some cellists come as close as anyone in the interviews to displaying the clear discrepancy between the realities of playing in an orchestra and the ideals of their early years. They articulate their career discontent with such phrases as "I never wanted to work in an orchestra," "it never impressed me," "it's a waste to spend your life playing in an ensemble," or simply, "you have to be realistic." This picture of the orchestra, with variations from case to case, is in clear misalignment with the personal stake in a calling as soloist or chamber ensemble (particularly string quartet) performer. In trimming their sails, they come to realize the structure of opportunities in the music business open to them and their own limitations of ability and motivation. For those interviewed, it seemed as if the orchestra was, at best, something to fall back on in the face of these problems. In this sense, it was a form of career insurance, a line of defense reducing some of the hazards of their careers as musicians. It was also a type of choice which allowed

6. Howard S. Becker and Blanche Geer, "Latent Culture: A Note on the Theory of Latent Social Roles," *Administrative Science Quarterly* 5 (September 1960), 304-313; John Irwin and Donald R. Cressey, "Thieves, Convicts and the Inmate Culture," *Social Problems* 10 (Fall 1962), 142-155; Rose Giallombardo, "Social Roles in a Prison for Women," *Social Problems* 13 (Winter, 1966), 268-288; David A. Ward and Gene G. Kassebaum, *Women's Prison* (Chicago: Aldine Publishing Company, 1966); and John H. Goldthorpe, "Attitudes and Behaviour of Car Assembly Workers: A Deviant Case and a Theoretical Critique," *British Journal of Sociology* XVII (September, 1966), 227-244.

them to stay in music rather than relinquish completely their self-concept as performer, or face the difficulties in trying to step onto another career escalator relatively unprepared. Again, the distinction between career moves into the orchestra and going commercial are blurred. This is probably due to the retrospective accounts as well as to the rather prosaic outlooks of these musicians; that is, going commercial was viewed as a better bargain for the realization of such important side bets as earning a good living, supporting a family, and having enough time to do the things they "really" wanted to do. For the majority of musicians interviewed, career paths lead out of the symphony and into the studios before they were 30 years old.

Disenchantment and the Erosion of Orchestral Aspirations

In contrast to studio musicians who wanted to be concert artists and looked to the orchestra as a second choice, quite a few of those interviewed reported that they aspired to be orchestra musicians before their twenties. Three-fourths of the French horn, string bass, woodwind, and reed (oboe, bassoon, clarinet) players said they ideally wanted this career. Instead of being a setting for hedging career bets, the orchestra was a positive reference point on which they staked their reputations and skills. Making it into a position in the upper ranks of the orchestra world was a major career plan. By way of contrast, only a handful of violin, viola, and cello players reported that this career line was their first-choice or ideal aspiration.

What then leads so many of these musicians who looked to the orchestra as a primary career goal to abandon their early interest and move out of this setting? A complete answer would, of course, require a study of orchestra musicians who remain and those who do not.

Some partial answers are provided by our studio musicians whose responses bear a striking similarity to Westby's findings which emphasize the gradual erosion of occupational identity as a symphony player, discontent with one's economic situation in the light of the financial problems which hang over many of our orchestras, and the feeling of career entrapment.

A central difference in the perspectives of these commercial musicians emerges during their retrospective accounts of career movement. Some of them were enchanted by the orchestra, or what they thought the orchestra would be. Instead of a weak career choice, even a "cop out" or failure, this setting was portrayed not only as a prescribed career line, but a glorious endeavor. It was a calling. Thus the most bitter views of this calling were held by those who reflected on the sharp distinctions between the investment and effort put into this career, and the slim rewards received. I found few violin players using the strong language displayed throughout the interviews by performers who looked to the orchestra as the culmination of their dreams. The latter respondents link their move into the commercial setting to the failure of the orchestra; in contrast to solo aspirants, they attained their goals, but the concrete manisfestation of those goals — lack of pay, poor conditions of work — set up a wide discrepancy between principles and practice. This fracture increased their receptivity to possibilities of moving off the orchestra world's escalator. On reflection, they muster a great deal of indignation and feel cheated. While the violinist or cellist who wanted to be a concert artist sometimes had difficulty in richly describing how this career was thwarted — except for the broad outlines of problems with the music business — former orchestra musicians almost endlessly recounted the details of embitterment and the shattering of ideals.

There follow several lengthy excerpts from interviews with these musicians which illustrate the fracture between idealism and concrete orchestral problems. The first is a reed instrumentalist who is at the top of the most powerful contractors' hiring lists. His early ambition was to play first chair with a major symphony. Before his twenties he was well on his way to accomplishing this goal. The following response developed out of nearly one hour of discussion concerning the symphony itself. Asked why he became dissatisfied with a particular issue in his career, he replied:

I got disenchanted because here we were in the symphony pursuing *the* great art form, and yet, none of the orchestras were self-supporting. We weren't playing music for a great population, we were playing for a few, and particularly to the people who were handing the money to the symphony. They did it for reasons best known to themselves, but in many cases they were sure to be seen in their boxes every Thursday night. I'll give you some very specific disillusionments, and they didn't affect me so there was no bitterness. I looked at it happening to others, and it hurt me deeply. In that symphony, for instance, one of the donors — you see the symphony couldn't exist on its own income and most hadn't been able to get community help so they got "society" help — Mrs. X of the Z Company family decided to use her $10,000 to help the Opera Society. She figured they needed it more than the orchestra, so she took it and gave it to the Opera. Four violinists lost their jobs. Four violins had to be cut from the orchestra because of the $10,000. And I looked at those four and thought, "Well you're secure, they'll never drop you for funds, because the orchestra will go under first." So these four men, and their wives, and their families, and their livelihoods, and the years they had spent building up to this point, were gone. So they're out. Why? Not because they played poorly, not because the symphony failed, but because of a little bit of patronage. Well, there you go. That was one of my first disillusionments.

He went on:

My next disillusionment was, and this will have to be anonymous because it just shouldn't be known . . . the major orchestra, one that I had dreamed about since childhood, it was my aim in life. Their first chair died. And the conductor immediately offered me a position. I got so excited, I thought it was the greatest thing ever happened to me. And then he said, "By the way, I don't know what kind of salary they gave you in the X orchestra," so I told him and he said, "We don't have that kind of money." Then he offered me one-third less to go to this great orchestra! I looked at him and said, "But my grocery bills are going up every week" and he looked me square in the eye and said, "But think of the honor, the honor." Well, that was just about it. And the point is this: what is this great art of playing in an orchestra when you still have to go to the grocery store and buy a loaf of bread. And then they try to pretend that it's on a different level, it's on a different scale.

At this point, this musician got up and started for his study, he explained:

Now there's a very interesting article, I have had reprints made of it, the *Time* magazine came out with it a few weeks ago. Did you see it? People leaving the orchestra; let me get you a copy. People leaving to go elsewhere. This will fill you in on the rest of my disenchantment, because it's exactly what I've done. I have gone to get my musical enchantment back — I've gone into teaching and everyone is finding there's no musical enchantment in the studios. We earn money. And if a better score turns up in the studio, it's very happy and pleasant to work with it. But more and more musicians are beginning to find the great joy in teaching. And if you're a good teacher, you get the gratifications, more gratifications than playing in a symphony. It would be all right if you could play different music all the time in the symphony. But what can a guy think when he's going out to do the Brahms C Minor for the thirty-first time? The situation is changing now. It's how I refused conductor X's words about the honor of sitting in this orchestra. All I could see was that he's asking me to sit with honor for one-third less when a loaf of bread is costing more every week. Now what kind of ivory tower can I live in with that kind of theory? I know many say, "Oh, you're just commercial." But I'm not; I'm a realist and to-day's musicians *are* more realistic, their ivory towers are tied in with the cost of living. Does that make sense? This has been a little bit of a catharsis for me.

Again, the value of being a realist and the positive attraction of studio work in terms of monetary reward and time for teaching constitute the main features of this outlook. A major source of career dissatisfaction stems from what this musician calls the ivory-tower theory of making a living in the orchestra. The conductor and community sponsors are clearly the villains in this retrospective drama. Refusing to stumble along on a poor paycheck and disenchanted with the repetitive work schedules, this musician went commercial. This decision is conceptualized in very conventional terms; the commonly shared outlook gives priority to making a good living and using music almost like a business.

The next respondent makes this business type of adaptation even more explicit. More than any other musician interviewed, he returned quite a few times during the discussion of his career to the problems which forced him into studio work. There are references, both direct and indirect, to a set of beliefs which justify why musicians like himself must relinquish their status as devoted "classical" musicians. Like his colleague, he began with a profoundly skeptical picture of the orchestra and its audience.

People don't go to concerts to hear them, they go to see them. The better the dance the conductor does on the podium, the more of a success he is. The louder the sound, the more success it is. And I blame the public for that, not the conductor. The conductor wants to preserve his tenure, so he's got to cater to those who will support him. Anyway, I began to see that my fulfillment as a musician couldn't happen in that kind of an environment. The goal was not to play beautiful music and to play as well as you can. The goal was really to please the backers. So I found that I wasn't making too much money at that time, and felt that I could not fulfill my desires musically – and I sure as hell wasn't fulfilling them financially – so I might as well use music as a business. So there were only two places to go. One was New York and the other was Los Angeles.

Later in the interview he summed up his views about orchestral work:

To maintain a certain financial status which the musician finds necessary, they have to sell their birthright. And I don't blame them. I think my experience in the symphony and experiences of my colleagues all over the country, all of them, only verifies the fact that symphony musicians are badly paid, vastly overworked, and underappreciated. It's revolting. So if we want to stay in music, we are pushed into the commercial end of it.

Along with issues of income, conductors, and overwork, the orchestra setting generates another, but related, set of problems. These center around the successful negotiation of career contingencies particular to the orchestra. The ambitious string, woodwind, reed, French horn, and orchestral brass player knows that his personal success and achievement are shaped by several structural properties of organizational careers in this setting. A most important feature is that the very best is of considerably more stature and prestige than merely the best. In terms of wage scale, length of season, status, and level of musical performance, there are relatively few positions for the aspiring performer who wants to make it into the elite command posts of the orchestra world. Principal or second chair positions in the top five or six orchestras such as the Cleveland, New York, Boston, Philadelphia, and Chicago comprise the upper rungs of this career ladder.

The musician traveling this career route encounters

several types of occupational risks. Metaphorically speaking, the orchestral escalator is slow-moving; there are many colleagues and potential competitors on it, and career footholds must be established quickly if one is to move upward. For example, the recruit runs the risk of starting too low on the career ladder; he starts in the minor league orchestras and fails to climb fast enough into the celebrated ranks. Since most high-status symphonies are generally reluctant to hire anyone over 35, his career fate can be decided by the mere passage of time out of the big leagues. On the other hand, he may move into the upper ranks, but then subsequently fail to move up in his respective section into the principal or second chair, or in the case of the strings, into the concertmaster, first or second stand position. Thus while being higher on the career rungs, he will be "frozen" or trapped within the internal status structure of the orchestra.

In looking back, a number of string players exhibited this last pattern. They had bet the improvement of their life chances on remaining in the orchestra and on following the culturally prescribed, traditional career path that was supposed to lead up into the top ranks of the string section. This side bet committed them to a future line of action which, several candidly acknowledged, eventually constrained them from moving to another, and perhaps more economically advantageous, place in the music business. Here is a musician who spells out this feeling of constraint that came when he felt obligated to pursue his career in a famous, high-status orchestra. Asked if he would follow a similar career if he had it to do all over again, he said:

> I doubt it. I would never have stayed in the B Orchestra for that number of years. It would have been smart to stay there for maybe four years or so, to learn the repertoire and get the experience of playing in a symphony. The rest was a mistake.

I guess I was fearful of leaving. I guess I thought that being part of one of the world's great orchestras, I should be proud to be in it. But this is false actually. You're not going anywhere, you're not doing anything, and you're stuck with a small salary. You feel trapped. You feel as though you've achieved the top of your field; and you have more or less. But there's not too much satisfaction going along with it. It's better to have a little more money and a little more freedom for things that are more satisfying musically. So, I moved out here.

In this case, career entrapment centers around the fact that the musician staked too much in his perspective, and lost the chance to make other valuable bets. He bet the improvement of his career, in this case, on the climbing process — on moving up within the section. But like his colleague's response above, the disjunction between status and money, between expected and actual acquired valuables, increased the attractiveness of other lines of activity. Reinforcing the feeling of "not going anywhere" were the familiar set of work problems and little off-the-job freedom for chamber music and other leisure interests. Rather than settle into a position near the top of his string section, and rather than face the eventually slow movement onto the first stand, he preferred to face the hazards of moving to Los Angeles in hopes of making it into the studios. After a few years of breaking in, he became a regular in the inner circle and very active in the concert scene.

It is probable that many orchestral aspirants, as well as those who wanted to be concert artists, had scarcely begun to build up valuables likely to commit them to the symphony as a career. The erosion of orchestral aspirations occurred before their mid-twenties. Unlike their colleagues above, accumulated time on the symphony promotion ladder and the feeling of shutting off potential sources of reward were not predominant in their outlooks.

Their sense of entrapment was not as deep or profound. Nevertheless, the outlines of this perspective can be found in their retrospective accounts. Disillusionment with a slow career climb or the possibility of getting trapped in the minor leagues of the orchestra world were mentioned by several players. The next two interview excerpts are illustrative of this. First is an interview with a gregarious woodwind player who, after two seasons with a middle-status orchestra, decided to return to Los Angeles where he took his college degree. His language is representative of several of the younger musicians interviewed. The second respondent is a young violinist who just recently became a member of the inner circle through the sponsorship efforts of an influential composer-conductor. In both cases, little was to be lost by going commercial. In the first case, it was the escape from the orchestra and its routine work; in the second, the salvation of the stake he had in his own pride and self-esteem as a virtuoso concertmaster. Both come close to articulating a sense of comparative failure, for both emphasized the problems and occupational risk involved in setting aspirations at the level of becoming a concertmaster or first chair principal in a major orchestra.

We were discussing his career history when the woodwind player laughed and reflected on his recent move out of the orchestra:

> I played a couple of seasons in the D Symphony and then I broke my contract. I couldn't stand it any longer. The playing wasn't much fun and the money was very bad. I think I was making $75 a week and on top of that, the season was short. I survived, let's put it like that. The next year I was offered a contract with the B orchestra as assistant first at $20 more a week. I didn't want that either. Look, it's hard work. You're on the spot all the time and you can't relax. I broke my contract and came back here to do studio work, to have some

more time, you know. The orchestra is just like a nine-to-five job, no freedom, and so who needs it? I guess you say, "I'll be first in the New York Philharmonic," but you got to earn a living and you find that it might not work out and you have to recognize this.

The violinist cooled himself down and like his colleague placed emphasis on the idealized self-image many young musicians have of themselves and their futures. He said:

After those years in the conservatory I was looking for a concertmaster job in a major symphony, but I couldn't find much and honestly couldn't face the possibility of working in some damn bush-league orchestra for years and years. God, who would want to do that? It's death. Also, I didn't care to work for the conductor in the G Symphony and commercial work was very lucrative. So, that was it.

And a reed player summed up the reasons why he never moved into the orchestra setting in the first place; emphasizing the valuables built up in commercial work, reluctance to face the bush-leagues, and some regret at failing to follow the culturally prescribed career line, he said:

I was making more money in commercial work when I was nineteen than I think I could ever have made in *any* symphony in this country. I was trained to do it, to play in the orchestra, but I never did. The routine would be dull and all the time in the minor leagues, so to speak . . . no, not for me, not at all. You have to be practical and commercial work came along. . . . I guess I should have fought the urge to make money and gone into a symphony.

We can only speculate on some of the implications these outlooks have for the future of our orchestras. One striking trend appeared to be the cynical, or call it practical, view of many of the younger string, woodwind, and reed players (the majority of brass players interviewed were from the big bands, as were the saxophone players). They had less reverence for the climbing process involved in an orchestral career and a coldness towards looking at this as *the* only traditional and probably honorable way of living as a classical musician. In Los Angeles, particularly, a few things account for their cynicism.

First, and most obvious, would be the increasing visibility of commercial employment in the recording, motion picture, and television industry. Certainly some of the best musicians in Los Angeles are found working in the studio salt mines. Many are also active in teaching and, eventually, in sponsorship of their higher voltage protegés. Reinforcing this trend is the fact that several of the performers in the Los Angeles Philharmonic are very active studio players. In fact, it was often noted in some of the career histories that one way of coming to the attention of colleagues and contractors was to play in the orchestra as well as in the "casual" concert scene around town. The attraction of the studios also pulled away potential talent from the orchestra, creating, as one can imagine, an interesting situation where the talents of the best musicians in town can be found playing jingles and television commercials rather than Beethoven or Telemann. And the second trend documented here is the economic crisis which burdens the majority of orchestras in this country. As reflected in the interviews, the push out of the symphony for prosaic monetary reasons is just as important as the potential attraction of commercial work. Hopefully the reader has by now some understanding of why musicians feel entrapped and move out of orchestras after only a few years of career climbing, or never set foot on this escalator in the first place.

Stable Careers and Comparative Success

While many string players failed in their attempts not to become orchestra musicians and many who aspired to this career became discontented with the tedium and low ceiling of concrete rewards, a sizable number of respondents reported that they aspired to be successful studio musicians or that they attained the top of one musical career ladder and then moved onto the higher rungs of commercial employment. With the majority of trumpet, trombone, saxophone, and percussion performers, the move into the studios is seen as a positive one, consistent with early career dreams. The chance to settle down in Los Angeles is not compared to what they might have done if things were different in the concert field or in the orchestra world. The studio career is viewed, in contrast, as a positive accomplishment in itself, more as a goal achieved than a grudging sacrifice to economic necessity.

Most of the musicians interviewed who played brass, saxophone, and percussion instruments had career lines which passed through the famous big bands of the late thirties and forties such as those of Glenn Miller, Woody Herman, Claude Thornhill, Stan Kenton, the Dorseys, Bob Crosby, Les Brown, Harry James, etc. All the brass and saxophone players were first or second chair musicians in these ensembles, some were featured soloists with heavy reputations in the jazz field when they moved into commercial work. In contrast to string players, and most woodwind-reed respondents with orchestra background, their retrospective accounts emphasize that the dominant valuables to be found in commercial work were not only *remunerative* but also *musical*. In the accounts of string players, the career choice of studio work is completely devoid of emphasis on improving one's skills or sharpening one's talents. With former big band musicians, the nexus between studio work and developing as a performer is frequently spelled out in detail. Not a few mentioned that work in the studios was a step up, both economically and musically. They bring to their commercial employment a different set of reference points. And while the familiar outlines of getting off the road and of building a family are major attractions of the high-wage employment in Los Angeles for those who make it, the musicians are often more excited about the uses to which their skills are put.

A few illustrations of these points follow. The first is from an interview with one of the studios' top brass players; after several years of nightclub gigs, he finally broke into the big bands and worked his way into one of the most famous bands. During the War he played in the service after gaining a foothold in the studios; after the War he returned to Los Angeles and has been a solid member of the inner circle ever since. He evaluated the steps into studio work in the following way:

> In the days of the bands, under the road situation, which was no joy with all the traveling, after you made it in the bands, the next step was commercial music, either in New York or out here. That was *it,* that was the *top.* You can't go any higher. Now, I've seen many of those players not make it in studio work out here. They weren't versatile enough or couldn't play all the music. Let's face it, it's much more demanding than just pounding out a band arrangement. You got to be smart, flexible. I felt lucky to be able to work here. Financially, I'm at the top of the business, and there's no further way to go for me musically.

This musician is clearly a comparative success; he has made it while others have not; moreover, he compares his own abilities with those who could not meet the demands of the recording sound stage. Much of this we have already seen in some interviews with string players; again the emphasis is upon meeting the work pressures. Unlike those players, however, he is not evaluating his present situation either in terms of "being realistic" or of past aspirations. He has attained both an extrinsic (in terms of money) and an intrinsic (in terms of performing skill) plateau. His commitment, then, to studio employment is broader and not nearly so monetary as many of the former orchestra musicians or aspiring soloists interviewed.

Here is a top studio percussionist who reached his career aspiration before he was 23 years old; being "realistic" meant that he went on to something better. The nexus between expectation and realization is tight; this is something that is missing in almost all the interviews with string players. Here we were talking about his career history:

> When I was in the bands during the thirties and forties, I figured that . . . well. . this was it, this was my dream, what I'd always wanted to do – to be a drummer in the bands. Buy by that time I had gone about as far as I could in them, especially after playing in the greatest bands around. So I said to myself, "You can't do this all your life; you've got to go another way," and I did, I got into studio work. I've been fortunate and lucky, really, to move from the bands into the studios, with little or no break at all.

The possibility of entrapment on the road and increasing age rendered many of these big band players available for other lines of action. As they grew older, much of the fun went out of these experiences, income was not significantly balanced with increasing familial responsibilities, and the fear of comparative failure loomed large in their perspectives. Several noted that they started on the road very early in life and were simply not enthusiastic about gambling the improvement of their life chances on a setting they had been in for so long. Many reflected on these earlier days as times grew out of; however, they directed little bitterness at the music, leaders, or other musicians in the big bands. These were clearly good times that could be enjoyed when someone was young. After a while, the point of diminishing status and economic returns sets in. Here is a saxophone player who was a soloist with a famous·organization; we talked about the role marriage had in his decision to come to Hollywood:

> It got me off the road. I settled down. And we got down to studying and staying in one place, trying to make it in one place as a studio musician. I think if I hadn't gotten married, I would have gone on the road longer. I was 24 and I had been on the road for about—well, since I was 16 and I felt it was time. I didn't want to wake up some morning and be 35 and still on the road, and I'm not kidding; there were a lot of guys that age on the road when I was a kid. There's no future, just going from one one-nighter to another. I never could see that.

Here is a colleague who also could not see a future in the big bands; after several successful years during the forties with some famous organizations, he moved into the Los Angeles contract scene. His reflections about the symphony orchestra are particularly interesting:

> I wanted to get out of the bands because I just didn't like the traveling or the idea of going all over the country and seeing the back door of every city, going through the kitchen and all that crap. That's all right when you're a kid, but when you get a little older you don't get a kick out of it any more. You want to settle down and raise a family you can't do that when you're on the road. You know, after a while it gets to be a real drag: bad hours, getting drunk, working all the time. It's like working in a factory. I guess I could have gone into a symphony, but that's death . . . dull . . . it *is* a factory.

The fear of staying "too long" in the bands, the potential erosion of success in terms of this shared conception of career timing, and the growing lack of status rewards admittedly increased the attractiveness of moving out of the bands and going commercial. The musicians perceive and react to moving into the studios and their current work situation in terms of these past experiences. Their frame of reference places value not only on money but on an interweaving of status, better music to play, more versatile and skilled colleagues, and security for their families. Having achieved a desired level of recognition, they look forward to, in their words, "the next step." And that step was upward in mobility. They do look back, however, at some of the features of the past they avoided or surpassed, such as colleagues who failed to move up the career ladder as fast as they did or who stayed for many years on the circuit. More than the string players who aspired to be soloists, and former orchestra musicians, the studios were indeed a very good thing for many reasons. And a typical career concern of musicians before they moved into commercial music was a shift in reference and aspiration point to other musicians, some of them former big band colleagues who were then working in the studios. These studio musicians became desirable models for the next rung on the ladder, which centered around gaining a foothold in the studios rather than climbing as fast as possible.

Specific past experiences shape a player's outlook on going commercial. A number of brass, saxophone, and percussion players aspired to play in the studios as an ideal career by their twenties; hence, for them studio work was a realized goal. For others, the connection between past shared experiences as musicians and current situations was not as close, but neither would it be accurate to characterize this transaction between past and present as a clear-cut dichotomy. Good examples of the relation between past experiences and present situation are the jazzmen and former jazzmen interviewed. While they value money and wealth, going commercial is more than simply a pragmatic resolution to some conflict between "musical" *versus* "monetary" rewards. If it were, they would give absolute priority to exclusively maximizing economic returns at the expense of their former musical ideals;[7] but accommodation rather than conflict is a pervasive frame of reference.

Rather than a sharply demarcated boundary, this kind of hybrid orientation centers around a link or coupling found in the interviews not only with jazz musicians, but also with a broader range of performers. Their abiding outlook is one of a calculative synthesis of economic pay-off in the studios and the more intrinsic, and expressive, rewards both on and off their recording calls. The threads of idealism and a remunerative outlook run throughout these interviews; several players pointed out that being active on the jazz scene can, in fact, complement rather than conflict with career advancement in studio work. Recent trends, for example, in the Hollywood recording setting indicate that as younger jazz-oriented composers penetrate the studios, they will write for, request, and perhaps actively sponsor the player both versed in commercial skills and blessed with jazz talents. Increasingly, jazzmen are solidly in demand by contractors and make up part of the inner circle. In this connection there probably is a fusion between bringing one's name before a wider audience of colleagues, composers, and contractors and career success. Also, playing jazz is a way of sustaining an established reputation. It is a type of occupational insurance built by spreading one's reputation and accounts with significant people in a wide array of available work in Los Angeles. In this respect, the performers interviewed display a wider variety of skills and have a wider span of potential jobs "covered." In contrast to Becker's description of narrowing skills to fit a wide variety of jobs,[8] studio performers are more broadly gauged in their virtuosity and craftsmanship.

7. This is the impression I get from Becker's argument in "Careers in a Deviant Occupational Group," *Outsiders* (New York: Free Press of Glencoe, 1963), Chapter 6.

8. Becker, *op. cit.*, p. 113.

Rather than the grim fight against what Becker calls "outside demands," free-lancers do not give up absolutely all aspirations linked to jazz and scale their expectations down to be more in alignment with the commercial situation. The availability of club and concert work outside of the studios, plus jazz dates at the recording compainies, set the stage for easy movement between the roles of studio player and jazzman. In the words of one respondent, "free-lance allows me to split the difference." And this is the difference between the rewards of both roles.

Such a fusion is a variant of the familiar Jekyll-and-Hyde theme — minus the degradation of the commercial side — introduced by many of the former orchestra musicians and aspiring solo concert artists interviewed. New performers do not overlook the net advantages of the Los Angeles scene and the number of brass, saxophone, and percussion players who share the experience, or who believe in "splitting the difference." Many of the younger players, for example, are more likely to adopt commercial outlooks when it is presented as compatible with the pursuit of their own career interests. Certainly this is the pattern for those who came from the big bands, and who are now studio regulars and members of the inner circle.

Several of the jazz-oriented players have begun to gradually shift their aspirations in the music industry to a different, and from their perspective, more creative terrain. They are now studying serial composition as well as the techniques and language of film scoring; eventually they hope to make it as composers. Some are already successful and are writing scores for rock-and-roll dates and some television film scoring. Many of the free-lancers interviewed mentioned this career line as something they would like to attempt in future years, ideally having composing, arranging, and conducting absorb more of their time than performance.

Some Implications

Going commercial obviously has different meanings for different musicians. For some the experience is essentially compatible with their aspirations; many, in fact, aimed to be commercial players early in life. Their success in the studios was, to put it simply, an extension of previous career experiences, the next step up on the career ladder. Thus, from the start of their careers, they appear to have a set of expectations and perceptions essentially consistent with what they experienced in commercial playing.

For other musicians, the move into commercial work is set against past expectations and experiences. They entered it to avoid some of the lower and slower net rewards of playing in the orchestras or the impossibilities of sustaining a successful career as a solo artist. Their outlooks and shared conceptions of studio work are, on the one hand, interwoven with references to dreams that were not realized and, on the other, bitterness of following prescribed career lines which failed to pay off in economic or musical advantages. When they look back, the fracture between dreams and deeds emerges in contrast to the majority of performers with careers in the big bands.

Career crises or recurrence of past events to be avoided at all costs are linked to historical conditions, and many of these respondents justify the pressures which forced them to go commercial in terms of past indignities.[9] Interviews with the old studio pros indicate that the experience of the 1930's had a great impact on their outlooks. This was a particularly difficult time for the older string players, who moved quickly into commercial work in theaters, radio, etc., rather than face the futile attempt to become a con-

9. This paragraph borrows from Alvin W. Gouldner's brief discussion of "paradigmatic experiences" found in his *Wildcat Strike* (New York: Harper & Row, Harper Torchbook, 1965), pp. 165-166.

cert soloist or chamber ensemble player. Clearly these were difficult times, but they earned very good livings throughout this period. More than any others the memories of these respondents were vivid when accounting for their decision to go commercial.

As an aside, occupational studies, and especially research in the sociology of careers, which neglect the historical context of decisions – particularly the Depression – are likely to overlook some of the recounted fears in subjects' past lives which shape their responses, both to our questions and to their own present and future experiences. For those with an orchestra background, the experiences to avoid are those which evoke images of "bad times" in the symphony. The priority they give to remunerative rewards, family security, spacious and comfortable houses in the San Fernando Valley, and "artistic" playing or dedicated teaching on the side have to be set against their efforts to prevent the recurrence of such "bad times." Thus, their current activity in the inner circle as successful studio free-lancers is, to use Gouldner's discussion of paradigmatic experiences, "fundamentally aimed at obviating another such traumatic experience."[10]

While economic motivations play a predominant role in luring performing musicians away from "high culture" work organizations to higher-wage competitors such as the studios, it should be noted that many of these respondents were, from the outset, somewhat reluctant to work in the orchestra setting. For some it was a mistake, an admission of comparative failure for not being "high culture" soloists. Others were reluctant because they wanted to occupy positions at the head of their respective sections, and they wanted to do this relatively early in their lives. Still other forces are here also: hard work, many

10. Gouldner, *loc. cit.* p. 166.

"services," long hours, and again, low pay. A few held out, gambling increased age against the possibility of receiving more money and becoming the top player in a section.

In a recent article, Herbert Gans sums up much of the attraction that commercial work has for artists. Framing the issue in terms of the pull away from "high culture," he writes:

> If one looks at high culture from a strictly economic perspective, it may be described as a low-wage industry that loses some of its workers to high-wage competitors and hopes that the rest will be satisfied with the spiritual benefits of low-wage employment. Given the affluence of the rest of society, the spiritual benefits that were once attractive no longer suffice, resulting in a shortage of high-culture creators.[11]

Some of the studio musicians would question the assumption of spiritual benefits; none would question the higher wages.

The folk notion of selling out and going commercial turns on this idea of sacrificing one's integrity for the pursuit of higher and quicker economic net returns. One difficulty with this approach is that it generally focuses only on one side of the dynamics of career choice; that is, it is exclusively concerned with what *pulls* the musicians into the commercial scene. This overlooks the very substantial forces which *push* the respondent off one career escalator and onto another. This chapter has been devoted to some of these latter features.

Another difficulty stems from the perspective that critics of commercialism (even "mass culture") employ. This might be called the "either-or emphasis." Either one goes commercial or one is an artist; you either sell out or you

11. Gans, *Social Problems: A Modern Approach*, ed. H. Becker (New York: Wiley, 1966), p. 559.

don't. A bridge between the two, a kind of hybrid orientation, centers around a more generalized coupling: on the one side, the virtues of craftsmanship, technique, and competence; on the other side, the values of creativity, expression, and artistic purity. While jazz musicians, to take a familiar example, outside the commercial scene may condemn this synthesis as a sell-out, and many in fact do in considerably more expressive language, they are emphasizing a narrow and rather inflexible set of orientations which they claim permeate these musicians' outlooks. The extremes noted by Becker of "playing what you feel" and "playing what the people want to hear" (or what you are hired to quickly and efficiently record) borrow much of the same emphasis.[12] By driving these opposites too far, I think both the jazzman and sociologist—in this case the same person—can too easily assign rather inflexible perspectives to musicians in the commercial setting in toto. He can also commit the error of assuming other performers hold values similar to his own. In the light of the respondents' shared outlooks and accounts for going commercial, more is concealed than revealed by conceptualizing this career move in such sweeping terms. Several assumptions in Becker's work, however, provide a comparative point of view for generalizing about going commercial.

While Becker admits the limited range of the commercial players he talked to and played with, he was satisfied that he had "enough contact" with studio players on staff at radio and television networks in order to discuss their outlooks towards their work and careers.[13] He recommends his work as an accurate description of the hierarchy of jobs from the lower-status, casual gigs to

12. Becker, *op. cit.* p. 108.
13. Becker, *op. cit.* p. 84.

the top staff orchestras. Nevertheless, his inferences
about the type of work performed, face-to-face
client-"practitioner" problems, and career stages appear
firmly grounded in the lower and middle levels of this
occupational hierarchy.[14] From the members' own frame
of reference, going commercial implies a "sacrifice of
self-respect and respect of other musicians," for these
settings present concrete problems, such as the in-
terference from the ignorant laymen, the probability of
doing the same tunes night after night, the low status *vis a
vis* colleagues in better paying and musically more rewarding jobs (the local scene), and the feeling of comparative
failure as judged against their more illustrious role models
(the cosmopolitan scene).

Certainly Becker is correct in pointing out that in these
casual work settings the goals of improvisation ("playing
what you feel") and artistic integrity conflict with the
interests of an audience seeking Saturday night entertainment and danceable music. This, moreover, an emphasis
on particular types of musicians; his description probably
includes pianists, bass players, drummers, brass players,
saxophonists, and some single reed players. A strong case
could be made for the argument that they have failed to
attain the success and recognition desired in the field of
jazz, and that they are comparative failures in terms of the
leading, charismatic figures in that special world.

Moreover, they may be second-rate technicians and
studio virtuosi, as well as second-rate jazzmen. This
double failure no doubt compounds their resentment in
having to survive on the lower rungs of the commercial

14. Becker's observations are derived from his experiences as a
piano player working in the casual settings of taverns, bars, and
various "jobbing bands"; his work role significantly influenced his perception of the occupational structure and the typical work and career
problems faced by its members.

world. And some of the musicians Becker knew were obviously at different stages of their careers; some were on their way up into the studios, others possibly were on their way down from the middle levels. We may expect bitterness about the commercial experience to be especially severe at this stratum of the music business. Without having the comparative data that would be required to develop this proposition, we do find a comparable resentment among free-lancers who, having gambled their life chances on going commercial, have not experienced many rewards, either musically, financially or in terms of social honor.

Becker's hypothesis about the role and career problems of going commercial are probably maximized under the structural conditions he describes. Several comparison groups within the Los Angeles studio structure were studied in hopes of increasing the scope and limiting the generality of this substantive theory.[15] A set of sensitizing concepts emerged from the interviews and field work, such as experiencing commercial work as a "runner-up occupation," "no other place to go," "a step up," and the collateral ideas of "Jekyll-and-Hyde outlook," "splitting the difference," and "studio work is the greatest." More general concepts are presented in this chapter as they emerged from the research experience: comparative failure, career congruity, prior orientations and entrapment.

Comparisons can be made within the sample of musicians interviewed as well as between these findings and Becker's. At the outset, a broader range or career backgrounds, aspirations, frames of references, and occupational structures can be located. First, Becker leans heavi-

15. The value of clarifying and assessing comparative studies is developed by Barney G. Glaser and Anselm L. Strauss in *The Discovery of Grounded Theory* (Chicago: Aldine Publishing Company, 1967).

ly on the work structure found in Chicago and Kansas City where he was a playing musician. The shape and height of the stratification system in Los Angeles and New York, as noted, is somewhat different from that in Chicago and Kansas City. This has several important implications. The greater volume of film, phonograph recordings, and commercial transcription work sets up a distinct strata of jobs in Los Angeles; the top of the hierarchy, in short, is composed of a different structure of opportunities. Moreover, the attraction of musicians to both coasts has a direct impact on the ratio of actual to potential members. For example, the small number of members in the elite inner circles of studio work in New York and Los Angeles—relative to those who satisfy the performance requirements—probably intensifies the struggles of recruits of all ages to make it, increases the role of sponsorship, and heightens the pressures of performance once the trials of breaking in are negotiated.

Second, and related, Becker's field work tends to focus on accounts of jazzmen; thus it limits the wider range of types of musicians and career lines found at all levels of commercial work, whether it be in Nashville, Kansas City, Miami, Chicago, Dallas, New York, or Los Angeles. Many musicians come from orchestras, some from big bands, others from the jazz circuit, and others up the ranks from casual dates such as Bar-Mitzvahs, cocktail clubs, bars, taverns, etc. This chapter has described what seems to be the entire range of backgrounds of studio free-lancers who are in the inner circle. Some parallels between free-lancers and Becker's jazzmen might be noted. String players who aspired to be soloists are in ways much like his jazzmen who went commercial. Both, for example, are comparative failures, and both look upon their present work as a sacrifice of artistic freedom and integrity. Both, moreover, find it necessary to cool their aspirations down and move off the more illustrious slopes inhabited by their heroès, be they Charlie Parker, Miles Davis, or Heifetz, Stern, and Menuhin. In both settings (Becker's and this one), one finds second-rate jazzmen, and probably second-rate soloists, but very few second-rate technicians and craftsmen, except at the lower rungs of the casual scene.

In the context of a broader range of career backgrounds and a different structure of jobs in the Los Angeles setting, Becker's conclusion about control of recruitment being in the hands of "cliques of jazzmen" is misleading. The colleague group which controls competition and regulates sponsorship is composed of a broader range of players, as one can infer from their backgrounds. As a collateral notion, then, those who have made it in the studios and who control the structure of the setting with contractors, composers, and leaders are not imbued with feelings of sacrificing "artistic ends" to commercialism. As a concrete example, the young recruit breaking into a brass section will be looked over by not only some players with jazz backgrounds, but by lead players out of the big bands, and by some former orchestra musicians, as well as by probably quite a few younger competitors who have moved up the ranks from casuals and rehearsal bands to recording work. As a side note, Becker does not devote a great deal of attention to climbing the hierarchy of available jobs, or to the movement away from the "lesser" work found at the lower strata of the business. He is most concerned with cliques, sponsorship, and breaking into a particular circle of players rather than with the more diverse networks of musicians stratified throughout the rungs of the career ladder. This has some implications for what going commercial means from the perspectives of various performers.

Unlike Hollywood studio free-lancers, Becker's players

define their situation largely as a move off the jazz scene into (or "back down" to) "routine" jobs. Their colleagues at both this lower set of rungs as well as at the middle levels are a various lot. To be sure, many of them are aspiring jazzmen, some of whom have the potential of making it, while others have failed and see going commercial as a demotion of sorts. Still others have failed in realizing their aspirations of becoming more than just "casual players" and never rose out of the cocktail circuit. This is clearly not the image of occupational life evoked by free-lancers in the inner circle, except as they reflect on the dirty work they were forced to do before their break came and the climbing process began.[16] (Opening breaks and movement away from low-status jobs will be examined in the next chapter.)

Rather than "putting down" or discounting[17] Becker's substantive theory of commercial musicians, the aim here has been to develop his insights through the use of a comparative framework which qualifies his findings to fit a particular set of structural conditions as well as suggest some new hypotheses and data on the problems of comparative failure and going commercial.

16. In another context Goffman has nicely spelled out the relationship I have in mind between structural position and outlook: "Persons at the bottom of large organizations typically operate in drab backgrounds, against which higher placed members realize their internal incentive, enjoying the satisfaction of receiving visible indulgences that others do not. Low placed members tend to have less commitment and emotional attachment to the organization than higher place members." Erving Goffman, *Asylums* (New York: Doubleday and Company, Inc., 1961), p. 201. In this respect compare my description of the work in the studios (Chapters 5 and 6) with Becker's discussion of "casual" work.

17. For a discussion of routine discounting procedures, see Barney G. Glaser and Anselm L. Strauss, *Awareness of Dying* (Chicago: Aldine Publishing Company, 1965), pp. 286-293.

CHAPTER FOUR

Making It in the Studios

Having looked at the career backgrounds, aspirations, and adjustments of our respondents, we now turn to some of the structural conditions of the free-lance setting itself which are decisive for the career success of these musicians. The informal channels of power and influence, the musical skills demanded of performers, and the distribution of social honor and prestige in the occupation all shape the system of social interaction in which careers develop. From the viewpoint of the free-lancer, these features are seen as problems to be solved, obstacles to be overcome, and conditions to be rendered as predictable as possible. They are occupational contingencies.[1] The successful handling of these features is called occupational success or, more informally, "making it."

The kind of career which a musician will have in the

___

1. Howard S. Becker, "Careers in a Deviant Occupational Group: The Dance Musician," in *Outsiders* (New York: Free Press of Glencoe, 1963), pp. 101-119; Oswald Hall, "The Stages of Medical Career," American Journal of Sociology LIII (March 1948), 327-336; and David N. Solomon, "Career Contingencies of Chicago Physicians," (unpublished Ph.D. dissertation, University of Chicago, 1952).

Hollywood studios and the degree of success that he will enjoy depend mainly on his ability and willingness to fit into the existing network of informal relationships among performers, composers, conductors, and the hiring contractors. Control over recruitment into the occupation and potential colleague competition are persistent problems. He is also faced with the tension and problems posed by the structure of recording technology. The starting point of this chapter is Becker's description and analysis of the career contingencies of commercial dance musicians. The setting described here, as indicated in the last chapter, is very different. Although Becker claims to have talked with performers occupying positions in radio staff orchestras and other studio work, his inferences about work demands and career problems refer mainly to free-lance players working in the middle and lower end of the job hierarchy in the Midwest, specifically Chicago and Kansas City.[2]

In contrast, this discussion focuses on a highly select "inner circle" of players who occupy positions of considerable status and power in the Hollywood studio setting. Several differences between these free-lancers and Becker's musicians are immediately apparent. First, the status of studio work is higher and the web of sponsorship and referral includes not only colleagues, but also composers, contractors, and conductors. Second, free-lance work presents these players with musical and technical demands which are more diverse and intense than those encountered by Becker's performers. And third, work problems for these players do not center primarily around face-to-face encounters with unknowledgeable and "square" clients or customers, but rather in some instances, with "square" producers, directors, composers,

2. Becker, *loc. cit.* p. 104.

conductors, and other studio staff. In addition, fads and fashions in musical styles influence what types and numbers of instruments will be used, as do production budgets, and the overall economic performance of the various film and recording companies. Studio players in Los Angeles display a wider range of career contingencies and work problems than are discussed in Becker's analysis.

Career Footholds and Getting In

When he seeks to enter the "inner circle," the unestablished recruit sees his career as contingent upon his ability to develop the proper web of contacts with those significant others who control access into studio jobs. Sponsorship is the major social mechanism which brings him to the attention of others, allows him to establish a reputation as a solid and dependable performer, and prepares him to cope with the various pressures of studio work itself. From the viewpoint of the sponsors, several important conditions must be met: (1) the young musician must be sponsored in such a way that established colleagues are not threatened with loss of power and privilege; (2) contractors and leaders must be convinced that the recruit is competent and can be depended upon; (3) the appropriate timing and pacing of the candidate's introduction into the division of studio labor must be determined and implemented; and (4) the candidate must learn the subtle etiquette of the referral system and, most importantly, must realize that sponsorship is a process of reciprocal exchange.

Breaking into the informal web of relations in the studios requires a combination of entrepreneurial zeal, aggressive self-advertisement, ability to handle interpersonal competition with grace and coolness, and performing talent. Several features contribute to the reputation a player is likely to acquire. Other people assess his ability to read music quickly and accurately, to play under pressure before audiences of colleagues, and whether he can be moved into the existing allocation of statuses or roles. The free-lance system does not directly allocate these to its members in clear and precise form, like an organizational blueprint. Members themselves assess their position vis-a-vis others in terms of the number of calls they get, the quality of the work call, and informal assurances by a contractor or contractors that they will be called by him.

An organized pattern is nevertheless identifiable, with those at the top of contractors' lists receiving the best-paying studio jobs. They comprise the inner circle. Those less in demand and farther down the lists occupy positions on the edges of the studio circle. "Breaking in," as the term implies, means waiting in turn for an opening, being sponsored, and successfully moving into the circle. To validate his commitment, the candidate must spend time working his way through the network of jobs in distinct circles made up of casual gigs, rehearsal bands, club dates, jobbing dance bands, orchestras, and so forth. In doing so, he indicates to significant others his willingness to undergo the ceremonial period of putting in his time. Implicitly he demonstrates to those behind him or to others just starting that he occupies a given position in free-lance work.

If breaking into the inner circle were simply a matter of putting in time, there would be a great deal of competition and hostility between musicians. Still, some recruits move faster than others, and some candidates get "frozen" at particular stages of their career movement into studio work. Sponsorship is the major mechanism for the regulation of human traffic from other free-lance work into the inner circle of the studios. The musician must come to the attention of significant inner circle members who can then actively recommend the candidate to other players and hiring contractors. This process is similar to the system of "tapping" found in the military and industrial management.[3] The sponsor sets the appropriate timing and pacing of the protege's entry and subsequent advancement.[4] Because considerable risk is introduced when someone is moved along faster than he "deserves," timing and a common sense notion of distributive justice (the correspondence between effort and reward)[5] are prime examples of the rules around which members orient themselves. Career timing is a function of the number of people whose career fates are affected by the introduction of a new member. Those solidly "in," who are at the top of the contractors' lists, have less to worry about than those on the edges of the inner circle. Thus, the sponsor must be careful not to move the candidate too quickly into these areas if he expects the reciprocal approval of his colleagues. The sponsor and protege have nothing to gain and much to lose if they fracture the link between the time and effort invested (in "getting in") and occupational rewards ("making it").

An example of the link between the etiquette of handling the perceived suspiciousness of colleagues and putting in considerable investments is an outgoing and gregarious brass player who discussed some of the problems involved in getting a foot on the inner circle ladder. He

3. Morris Janowitz, *The Professional Soldier* (New York: Free Press, 1960), pp. 145, 151.

4. Howard S. Becker and Anselm L. Strauss, "Careers, Personality, and Adult Socialization," *American Journal of Sociology* LXII, (November, 1956), 253–263; Norman H. Martin and Anselm L. Strauss, "Patterns of Mobility within Industrial Organization," in W. Lloyd Warner and Norman H. Martin (eds.), *Industrial Man* (New York: Harper and Brothers, 1959), pp. 88-89.

5. George C. Homans, *Social, Behavior: Its Elementary Forms* (New York: Harcourt, 1961).

talks about the "moral division of labor" and the casual "dirty work"[6] he did before beginning to ease into the "better" jobs of studio labor.

> You're called to work when work occurs. You can't sell yourself as a musician as you would something else, like I had a degree from such and such. Your fellow musicians recommend you here and there, they see if you can do the work, and if you can, pretty soon you get more calls. You know, you do Bar-Mitzvahs, dances, dumb things, but eventually you start doing better work in films, rock-and-roll recordings. So, slowly I would get called, somebody couldn't make it, somebody was unavailable. My first job was at X studio. The contractor liked what I did and from then on things built up.

Career development is contingent on proper movement into the existing arrangement of colleagues; this musician points out that this process is slow and dependent on the actions of others. A reed player who made it in the studios a few years ago talked about the problem of breaking into the division of labor and the importance of pacing and timing in advancement.

> You put in a certain amount of time before other players will recommend yo to the good jobs. I mean, I had to work my way into it. When you come into town as a strange musician, you gèt strange reactions, people don't want to just welcome you with open arms. You have to prove yourself and you have to run the gamut of suspicion from other players because someone thinks you're going to take jobs away from him. That has to be worked out. You can't be a threat to the established players; if it's your turn and you're called and nobody's being aced out, then there's encouragement and no resentment.

The most direct impact of informal organization on the candidate is in handling the rather diffuse contingencies of

6. Everett C. Hughes, *Men and Their Work* (New York: Free Press, 1958).

uncertainty: first, the problem of taking away someone's work, but, more importantly, incurring the dislike of significant others for doing so; and second, as a "rookie," the uncertainty of what will actually be the consequences on others of one's own advancement. Considerable apprehension also centers around the support a musician can expect from sponsors if he is seen as "moving too fast," or "acing someone out."

Colleagues are important in helping the sponsor move the protegé across the paths and plans of others into the existing network and in getting on with his career. But they are also potential exploiters. The etiquette of sponsorship forms part of what Hughes has called "[the] almost instinctive attempts of a group to cushion themselves against the hazards of their careers."[7] Colleagues are concerned about their own careers. They can resist or even "dump on" players by specific acts of neglect. The most apparent case of this is when a player attempts to break in without the explicit recommendation of another musician who performs on a similar instrument. After all, they reason, it is their own position that is being threatened. One of the most powerful members of the inner circle candidly described the appropriate ways of "making it." He then moved to some of the more unpleasant types of political maneuvering which can take place in free-lance work and the resources the inner-fraternity can bring to bear on these blatant attempts at career advancement.

Getting into this jungle is very, very difficult. You have to be very smart. Two things count. You have to have knowledge of your employers, who you are working for, the leader on the date, what they want, how best you can contribute to their music. The next thing is knowledge of the methods, the subtle methods, of contact in this work. One way is to play

7. Hughes, *loc. cit.* p. 108.

and be seen in bands, orchestras, wherever work is. You create your own product.

Some players come into town and try to undercut the guys already established out here; they don't survive one week, they're through before they start. You see, we know what's happening and how a guy is operating. If you're smart you'll get encouragement from other players; if you're not, forget it, you'll just cut your own throat in a hurry. For instance, some guys come into town, call up every goddamn contractor and say "A told me to call you, B said this and that, you know...use me...." And then on a date a contractor comes up to you and asks you if the guy was recommended by you. If we don't know him or didn't recommend him, well that guy's in trouble, and he'll have problems getting any work with us and the top contractors.

To the outsider, it might seem logical that if one is going to risk breaking into the inner circle, he might as well move in at its center rather than on the edges. However, this respondent indicates that there is more policing among the elite at the center than on the edges, and more power and influence to be exercised vis-a-vis hiring contractors. "Playing it smart" means knowing what the rules of conduct are and how they operate on all members in reducing the risk of free-lance careers. The free-lancer has the obligation to follow informal rules in regard to others; in turn, he has the expectation that others will cooperate as his advancement unfolds.

If sponsorship becomes widespread, all members become concerned because their informal positions are vulnerable. While many free-lancers in the inner-circle are reluctant to get involved in sponsorship, they share an interest in controlling the flow of recruits into their circle. Many do not actively sponsor because this involves not only putting a new recruit before their colleagues but also investing part of their reputation in doing so. This suggests that those who have the most influence and status with contractors and important others find it easiest to take such an active role in recommending new players. They have, in a sense, more social credit. But as a commodity of exchange, it can be used up quickly in the process of asking for preferential treatment for a protegé. This tends to depress the number of potential candidates. It also intensifies the critical importance of securing a foothold on the part of the sponsored musician. The fears of "blowing" a call, of folding up under pressure, of being unable to "cut" a difficult part were retrospectively recounted by many of the respondents. Relatedly, it is very important that the recruit live up to the expectation of his sponsor or sponsors.[8] Failure to come through reflects negatively on the sponsors' judgment, making others then reluctant to accept their future recommendations (if any).

Here is an interview excerpt with a young musician who is outside the inner circle; he explains a most dramatic instance of the failure to pass through an opening break set up for him by a powerful elite performer.

About three years ago, I met M at C Studios, he's a very popular player in the studios, very much in demand. He heard about my playing and later set up a date with me on it. It was handled very nice. He set it up with the contractors, arranged it with him and everything, he told the contractor I could do the job. I got the music a couple of days before the date. It was difficult and I practiced it four or five hours a day. It was full of up-tempos for a film they were shooting. He said it was easy and I would have no trouble. Well, it would have been easy for *him,* but not for me . . . at least not at that time. I didn't have any confidence in my playing. I backed out of the date. I just had to call him and say I couldn't do it. So he called the contractor and the contractor got pissed off at him and everyone got bugged with me. What a mess. If I could have done it, I would now be on call at that studio and into

8. Hall, *loc. cit.* p. 336

the scene, but I backed out at the wrong time and that was that. I've never got a call from them since . . . I can play that piece of music in my sleep now.

The significance of this episode is not the rather frank admission of being unable to play the music, but the fact that he was not able to play it according to his own standards of professional excellence. Undoubtedly some musicians do find themselves in these situations over the years. The point is the pressure of the call and the antici-pated consequences of mistakes under the studio micro-phones. He emphasizes how failure to handle these open-ing breaks can significantly slow down or ruin a career in the free-lance scene. This is because the network of spon-sorship, the connection between musicians and con-tractors, is dense, and the consequences of both good and bad studio performance quickly reverberate throughout the whole system.

Here is a young player who has been more successful than the musician above. He explains how he negotiated a similar terrain just a few years earlier. Clearly he was glad that the earlier period of pressure was over; he spoke of the critical moments of breaking into the inner circle, the sometimes painful lack of explicit encouragement given by non-sponsoring colleagues, and the pressures of always being prepared for uncertainty during a studio date.

The first job is the hardest, you're on trial. Nobody wants to hire someone for the first time unless they think you have a reputation. It's very hard for a new player to get in, but you got to be ready when the time comes, if you goof it, well . . . . This is something that players don't talk about, but they feel it, you know it's there and nobody says anything. It takes a pretty strong ego to put up with this pressure and the silence that goes along with it. The greatest fear in this busi-ness is the fear of the unknown. You never know what they're going to throw at you to play. So over a period of time you get a feeling of satisfaction that you're able to make it,

and it shows you've gone through the waiting, the pressure
and all of it. You never know whether you've made it or not,
no one says it. It's just the fact that you stood there on one
leg for so long and nobody told you you could put the other
one down.

This musician and the majority of respondents agree that
building a reputation is a difficult, pressure-filled, and often uncertain series of activities. Related to such contingencies are frequent expressions of frustration and annoyance about the uncertainty of success after having handled
their initial contingencies. The gradual approval of colleagues, an increase in calls, and the playing of more and
more calls with inner-circle members symbolize achievement in a musician's personal career. As the above respondent notes, there are no formal entrance criteria, cer-
tificates of "making it," or tenure. The major criterion is
how often one is called by contractors to work. The
player compares himself to others: he has moved ahead of
some, he is in competition with others, and still others are
more solidly in demand than himself. Such a system of
referral and the fluid criteria of success tend to magnify
the sense of injustice felt by those who have not yet made
it into the existing allocation of jobs or who have been left
behind with a lesser degree of success. Those on the
fringes or outside the inner circle of studio work in Los
Angeles have trouble intoning the joys of comparative
success. Predictably, the most common reason given for
their career fate has been the power possessed by contractors and the differential influence in sponsorship possessed by some free-lancers. Predictably, they save their
more open resentment for those in the inner circle: "the
all-stars who get all the work while the rest of us are
struggling."

The "all stars" and "cream of the crop" of the inner
circle are not the only free-lancers who actively sponsor

musicians. Composers and studio conductors frequently take an interest in moving a recruit along by putting pressure on contractors to hire him; and the more powerful the sponsor, the greater likelihood his efforts will be successful. This can create resentment among both contractors and performers. One string player, who shares with the other respondents an appreciation of the subtleties of hiring etiquette, reported how an influential composer-conductor, with many famous films to his credit, actively shaped the beginning of his career in Hollywood.

> I had been playing in various places and some of my good friends were composers and arrangers. One was instrumental in helping me. He told a couple of contractors to use me; you know the whole routine, "He's good, use him, help him." Well, being recommended doesn't automatically mean you're going to do all the contractor's work right away. It's hard to break into his steady group of people. But eventually I was used if some of the first players were busy, if they had other calls that day. I wasn't interested in cutting into their work and stirring up a lot of hostility. But eventually things started to fall into shape; I did the work, people liked my sound, and that was it.

This respondent points to the contractors' interest in perpetuating the existing informal organization of work and their implicit reluctance to bring new players in by hiring those performers with whom they are thoroughly familiar. The contractors have built up arrangements with this steady "stable" of players, and in handling their own work contingencies, turn automatically to these studio pros. With either a performer or composer-conductor for a sponsor, breaking into such an arrangement without creating enmity is an important part of free-lance etiquette, and a crucial career turning point.

These respondents suggest that there are different routes into the inner circle which are dependent not only upon one's skills and the power of the sponsor, but also upon the tightness or integration of a contractor's commitment to his stable of players, and the overall amount of studio work available to musicians. In other occupations, such as medicine, pool hustling, the academic world, and among Becker's dance musicians, colleagues exercise major control over recruitment and the pacing and timing of career advancement. Free-lance work presents a somewhat more complex set of roles. A prime example of multiple sanctions and influence is to be found in the various bargainings and agreements which go on among performers, contractors, composers, and conductors for musicians. This large number of actors elevates the uncertainty of a recruit's career fate by increasing the number of contingencies which he must handle. Thus, considerable intrigue, danger, and excitement reside at the beginning of his career moves into the inner circle; in addition, his actions and the actions of his sponsor affect many others.

Problems at Work and Personal Risk

Free-lancers must not only cushion themselves against the hazards introduced by colleague competition, but also must handle the contingencies of the work situation. The potential erosion of career success can come about because of the demands of studio work itself. These contingencies were summed up by nearly all the respondents in the epigram: "You're only as good as your last call."

Like policemen, reporters, doctors, and air-traffic controllers, free-lancers face unusual contingencies at work and must be prepared to handle a wide variety of uncertainties in performing their jobs. The established free-lancer, as well as the new recruit, must be in shape — both physically and mentally — for endurance, stamina, and concentration are demanded. One established player talked about some of the work and career strains; in doing so he developed the theme of supply and demand found throughout the interviews: "the contractor can always turn to other musicians."

> You get called for a date, the music is in front of you and you have to knock it off like that . . . right on the spot; read it immediately, and if you get into trouble, you've had it, and that's why we're there. You have to be ready and equipped, and have practiced, and be warmed up and you can't say, "Well, today I don't feel so good, I had a fight with my wife or I'm nervous or I had another call and I'm tired." The contractor doesn't want to hear it, the leader doesn't want to hear it. So there's a lot of pressure for the guy just breaking in, the clock is going and you're sitting with a 50-piece orchestra, and you're getting paid over 30 bucks an hour, it's expensive and there are these moments . . . if you can't do it there are 50 other guys waiting to have a shot at it.

The economics of recording, the continuous pressure to be ready to play anything, and the muted fear of colleague competitors were expressed most enthusiastically, if somewhat sarcastically, in the responses of some musicians. There is an obvious awareness and concern that the supply of musicians and eager recruits far outstrips the number of available work calls or positions on a contractor's list. Work pressures and career contingencies mesh; from the viewpoint of the musician, mistakes at work can lead to the contractor's calling other players whom he may regard as perhaps more competent. This would be a most dramatic instance of comparative failure and "demotion."

Along with these concerns, the musicians emphasize the considerable power of contractors in general. The contractors are viewed as important arbiters of what is a good performance, but most are not active performers themselves. In the musicians' discussions of contractors, there were few supportive statements. Contractors are viewed as ignorant and generally unaware of musical or artistic values and problems. These respondents sound like a group of jazz musicians discussing the problems with "squares" or rock performers complaining about "teeny-boppers."

Here is a brass player who explained the pressures of uncertainty on studio calls and how one can be only as good as his last performance under the microphones.

> You can't hide too long in this business. Composers write for all the stands and if you don't play much music one day, the next day . . . you never know, you might be on the first stand, and with a solo to play, and there you are. You either do it or you don't. You're continuously exposed, so you have to have good chops, stamina, everything right for each call. It's accepted that everyone have that, if not, they won't make it. Look . . . it's simple, if tomorrow I don't play well, the contractor might say "What the hell's wrong with him?" He'll never think of the last three years where you've never made a mistake. So you can lose it all in a day; I honestly believe it. You can come in a bar too soon, like you play a perfect recording and miss a note or page-turn and the guy looks up and says, "I won't use him anymore."

Even when a career is fairly well sustained, and when the musician enjoys considerable security, particular work problems can plunge free-lancers into traumatic moments. One of the most personally dramatic turning points was reported by an elder player. The incident involved a composer-conductor at one of the major studios and demonstrates how the musician sitting next to the player is a potential competitor. We were talking about the steps that led to his work in the commercial field.

> It was strange the way it happened. We were doing a picture and the first chair player was having trouble that day. The director looked over and said, " . . . you're flat, goddamn it,

you're flat and you know it, ever since we started this picture." Well, this guy gets up from his chair and goes over to the water cooler, gets a drink and the director says, "Are you ready to make this take now?" And he said, "I can't make it now, I'm so nervous." And I'll never forget that . . . he pointed to me and said, "You play first chair." And this take was a fast sequence, very tricky. I played it, that was it. I didn't realize it at the time, I didn't see the importance of it all . . . if I had missed that thing, well . . . I played it, not perfect, but well enough to satisfy the conductor I guess. We only made one take and he said "print it."

These free-lancers are among the more closely observed workers in our society, for their jobs are literally performances which are audible. Studio calls are precarious because, as one player put it, "We never know what they're going to throw at us." Each call is important; in most instances the players cannot practice their parts at home, as they can in the symphony orchestra. And for the established studio "pros" as well as for those breaking in, work problems put the contractors, composers, conductors, and colleagues continually on the spot. No one wants to be responsible for "clams" (audible errors). They are costly to the producer, and they increase the tension on subsequent takes for the work group. I should like to note that much of the music they are called upon to perform does not require them to use their skills, talent, and endurance to their upper limits. This, however, is in itself a major work contingency; the player must not let his skills slip or personally minimize the danger that some calls can present. A former orchestra musician summed up this theme, indicated how the contractor plays such an important role, and compared free-lance work to the orchestra.

You can go for weeks, months, without anything to play, just whole notes, dumb music. Then one day you walk into a call and have to play a solo. So you never stop being discovered and by God, you play it better than the guy who played it yesterday, and the contractor—who you've known for years—will say, "Boy, that sounds beautiful," you know, like, "I didn't know you could play that good." So you get called on and you better do it. That's one way of making a name and one way, I might add, of destroying yourself. You see, you're playing with some of the best musicians around. The challenge is to stay on top, to keep ahead of your instrument. There are many good players out here and the competition is tremendous. This is a completely different experience from what you go through in a symphony. It's very acute. Once you play your audition and pass your second or third year, you're there, you're in no matter how many people are waiting behind you. In this business you're only as good as your last call; only your last one. In many cases not even a second chance is allowed. I know of a couple of guys from an excellent orchestra who had some trouble with the dates at one of the studios, and that's it. That's all it took, just once or twice.

Despite the rather self-serving argument that while others have failed, he has made it, the implication is clear: a musician cannot rest on his laurels, at least not for long. Neither can he feign expertise, that is, come on strong as a backstage soloist, but fail to deliver when the red light for recording comes on. Contractors create additional risks for musicians. Performers acknowledge that invidious comparisons are made by contractors and that one can lose or gain work, move down or up the contractor's list, depending on his evaluation of the player. Again, considerable discretion is in the hands of the hiring contractor. A theme heard many times was that if "you're only as good as your last call," then "you're only as good as contractors think you are." Here is a musician who qualified this last statement, but endorsed it as a principle on which contractors operate.

It's a few mistakes and you're likely to be in trouble. You might find yourself not being called by that contractor, or

requested by that composer if you goof up his date. Word
gets around, for both good and bad jobs. It all depends. Some
guys say, "All right, he goofed but I know it was a bad day."
Others aren't so tolerant and say, "Why should I tolerate that
when there are fifteen other guys I can call who maybe won't
make any mistakes?"

The pattern of associated problems varies with position
occupied in the informal organization of studio work. The
more in demand by contractors and leaders, the more
work one can do, the more active one can be in bargaining
and sponsorship. Higher performance standards are often
expected of the elite players than for those further down
the contractors' lists. Within the inner circle, a select
group is called upon to perform the solo parts. This increases the pressure on them, for they have more at stake
than others. Successful handling of these contingencies
naturally heightens their market value. It also increases
the likelihood that others will request these "star" players.
This tends to strengthen the monopoly they already enjoy
while reducing the occupational risk inherent in this precarious system.

The conditions of informal organization, the power of
hiring contractors, sponsorship, and work problems are
each decisive in the success of the free-lance musician. At
any point in a career in this occupation, the ultimate
position of a member is problematic, due to features of the
work situation and its resultant system of social interaction.

Equally important are contingencies introduced by the
market situation and economic performance of the individual studios, the position of the industry in the economy, and more immediate concerns, such as the budget
expenditures for composers and performers and fads and
fashions in musical styles. Control over these external
features is largely out of the hands of the free-lancer. The

personal impact of these features differs depending on the individual's status in the informal hierarchy of studio work. To save space and compress the contours of this picture somewhat, there follow only two interview excerpts. First is a brass player very much in demand by contractors and composers. If he chose to accept all the calls he gets, he could work almost around the clock. He is in his mid-forties and has been successful in the scene for over 15 years. In this excerpt, he points to the importance of having many accounts, knowing many contractors, and being aggressive in going after calls. He comes closest to being the most intense rate-buster among all the musicians interviewed. He looks back, like other respondents, on the days following the contract orchestra and sees himself as a comparative success.

> You work according to what instruments a composer writes for, and if the studio gives the composer 17 men, he might not use my instrument, so I don't work that call. The big secret is to work for as many different people as you can. You have to spread your accounts. You may be first call with five, maybe ten, contractors and composers, which means when they put out a call, you will be asked for first. I'd just as soon be second or third call with 20 or 30 composers and a lot of contractors, which I think I am. I wish all the calls would fall into place one year. I think that's the trouble with a lot of guys, they get stuck in one place; they depend on one contractor, and when he falls through, or the studio goes quiet, they don't work. So you learn to juggle your dates, get around and be in demand. To be a success you have to be a businessman.

The next respondent is just such a free-lancer who was informally tied to one or two contractors. He has informal links to a studio which last year started to use fewer strings, which he plays, and more brass, percussion, and woodwind instrumentalists. Unlike his colleague above, he cannot muster much of an argument about the virtue of

aggressiveness and working for many contractors. When
he does refer to colleagues, he mentions the highly demanded "star concertmasters" with a bit of envy. He
nostalgically looks back on the contract orchestras. This
was clearly the best work and money he ever had in the
studios. Many violin, viola, and cello players who are not
in the inner elite circle of string musicians sound much
like this respondent.

> My work dropped off last year. The studio cut out my in-
> strument, so no violins were used. To have a violin section
> that sounds like anything, you've got to have at least six to
> eight players. The studio couldn't afford it for these series,
> they cut costs by reducing the section. They used a band
> instead.
> Q: What did you do then?
> What did I do? Nothing. You stay home and wait for the
> phone to ring, what can you do? I think cello is more popular
> now among composers, with four cellos you can get a sound.
> The big name concertmasters work, you know [he gives
> names of ten musicians] . . . mostly on the big productions,
> maybe some TV, but most TV doesn't use many violins or
> violas. Hell, I'm lucky if I can get a call once a week at X
> Studio.

Both musicians face problems inherent in free-lance
work. But the second respondent lacked a sustained series
of contacts with those who hire. The sure-fire entrepreneurial tone is unmistakably missing from his language. In
contrast, his colleague actively cultivated informal
influence and leverage with several contractors. In this
way he spread the risks inherent in this hiring network. By
building up his "accounts," he cushioned himself against
the fluctuations in studio productions, market demand for
various series, and potential colleague competition for
valued calls. Thus, those most in demand by others are
bound into a series of risk-reducing measures. By this I
mean they are involved in obligations to contractors

which involve a constraint to accept all of a contractor's work calls. The more in demand, the more one is a "star," the more irksome these bonds become. One way of achieving considerable freedom, then, is to be in the action with numerous contractors rather than with one or two very demanding ones.

The problem for members of the inner circle is to keep the system intact and moving toward its goal—in this case, the maximization of studio calls. From members' perspectives, a number of problems must be solved. Many of these problems are external to the inner circle, that is, they are not under the direct control of its members, for example, the market demand for films and records, and shifts in fashion which influence what instruments will be used and how often they will be employed. But the issue of who will work when a call goes out and who will play the most valued positions (both economically and musically) is a problem left mainly to the contractors and musicians themselves. The informal inner circle arrangement is a solution to this contingency.

In handling this problem, members offer an interesting instance of the sociology of occupational risk. Individually, a performer spreads his accounts and risks across a number of hiring agents. This is a privilege built into being a "star" in the inner elite. Collectively, members attempt to control the number of recruits into their circle. Sponsorship is the key mechanism of such regulation and it is typically exercised by those in demand positions. The career problems faced by the protegé or recruit, then, must be seen against the individual and collective attempts of inner-circle colleagues to build and sustain a form of social insurance, and to cushion themselves against the hazards of present and potential competitors, mistakes at work, and the precarious contingencies of free-lance employment.

CHAPTER FIVE

Skill, Dignity, and Flexibility

The studio musicians recognize that studio work requires them to maintain their skills at top capacity while, at the same time, they complain that the work they are called to do often frustrates the full use of their talents, and even their personal standards of excellence.

We find frequent expressions of discontent and annoyance with the writing of some composers and the pressures they put on the musician, and dissatisfaction with studio work is not solely a consequence of the job setting per se. It is in large measure part of an orientation towards work which musicians bring with them. Once in this work setting, gratification from the use of skill can be either heightened, sustained, or lessened. Also, there is a pervasive tendency for these performers to have great pride in their talents, characterized by a strong sense of individualism and autonomy. Their own internal standards of excellence and virtuosity lead to an orientation of craftsmanship and quality performance which tends to lessen the effects of the more "degrading" work situations found in motion picture, television film, and other recording settings.

Challenge and Monotony: The Pattern
of Work Contingencies

As outlined in Chapter 2, free-lance studio work is performed within a highly technical and changing work environment in which large sums of money are invested. Pressures and problems in this overall setting with which the musician must cope include the following: (1) the varying demands of the technology of film recording, including the precise synchronization of music and screen action as determined by the use of click tracks, microphones, etc.; (2) the demands which the music itself places on the performer's skill; (3) the ability or inability of the conductor to lead the players and coordinate their work with the screen cues; and (4) varying time pressures and production goals which create situations in which musicians can be called upon to use their skills at or near their peak capacity. Although film music is in many instances a secondary consideration in film production, mistakes made in recording are expensive, because they require resetting the film reel and other equipment, and starting again with another take.

Unlike the predictability characteristic of other occupations, free-lance work is irregular. For long periods of time the music will be routine. Most of the time everything goes smoothly. Occasionally crisis situations arise as mistakes are discovered in the music, when the recording balance is poor, when there is less and less time in which to finish a recording date, or when fatigue begins to erode a performer's technique, mental sharpness, and musical finesse. Some of these demands are a direct consequence of the technological setting rather than of the music itself, while others are tied to the individual performer's skills. Each reinforces the other.

One of the musicians began his discussion of the pressures of studio work by comparing it to symphony work and symphonic repertoire, and then went on to explain some of the sources of stress in recording situations.

I'd say that most of the time it's not Beethoven's Ninth or Schoenberg, but it has to be done quickly and I think one pressure is that there isn't too much margin for error. This recording light is on, the clicks are going, and you don't wish to be the reason for a retake. The conductor, I assure you, is under pressure. He is not thinking about you, he's worried about timing and the cues coming up so you got to do your best, you've got to come up to those standards. I'd say a certain amount of pressure is there because everyone expects a near-perfect performance all the time, right on the spot. They don't expect to do a piece of music too many times unless it's terribly difficult. So nerves are important, the pressure is within yourself, you're your own worst enemy or best friend.

Q: Time is important, I take it?

Sure, you go on a date and after a couple of takes you just don't make any mistakes; takes are very costly, and you have to deliver.

While much of the pressure in studio film recording is principally caused by technological factors in conjunction with the varying work demands introduced by composers and conductors, it is also supported by the hiring conditions of the industry. Musicians work when they are called by various contractors; although they can turn down certain types of work, once they have accepted a job they have virtually no control over what type of music they will play, or how difficult it will be. Moreover, they have little control over the pace of their work. Although union regulations provide for ten minute breaks every hour, the production personnel, music department, and conductor determine how much music will be done in the number of hours allotted for a call. One source of dissatisfaction stems from the speed at which recording takes place and musicians often complain that "we never have enough time to really practice a piece of music and get it perfect." Changing work situations at different studios with their various policies concerning music—"grind it out" or "take time"—add to the uncertainty of free-lance work. Each call has its own technical problems, musical difficulties, and time pressures; each represents a potential for crisis.

The alternation between *routine* and *crisis* seems to be characteristic of the film process and of its related technology in general, as well as a major contingency of free-lance work. One consequence of this changing work scene is the tendency to see work as both challenging and monotonous. Moreover, composers and conductors are also part of the film production process and they too are subject to further pressures introduced by producers, directors, and budgets. As a relatively minor budget expense, free-lance film work is closely tied to how much music the producer and others want, the status of the composer, his desires in orchestral instrumentation, the difficulty of the score, and finally, how much money is left for the music after the actual film shooting has been completed. These factors add unpredictability to the studio calls musicians find themselves on and to the demands placed upon their skills. From the performer's perspective, scores can be routine or challenging, depending upon the amount of time, effort, and creativity a composer has devoted to the music.[1]

One of the top cellists in studio work explained how this fluctuation magnifies the problems of boredom found

1. Percentage distributions of responses to "What type of calls are interesting most of the time?": Depends on composer, score, conductor, time for scoring, etc., 44; motion pictures, 28; both TV and motion pictures, 14; jingles, 1; all calls, 3; no calls, 4; other response, 6.

in commercial music where a score is often routine, stereotyped, and dull.

> Ninety-eight per cent of the time it's just simple and dull. But one or two percent . . . it's demanding and you have to do it. . . . Now tomorrow at 9:00 I have a call. I don't have the vaguest idea of who I'm working for, or what it is, or how big the orchestra is or who else is with me [in the section]. It may be X, Y, or Z studio . . . 9:00. Now a cue may come up from a cello concerto, which if Leonard Rose or Pablo Casals had for a goddamn concert, they'd have to study it for two months. And we have to knock it off . . . just like that, right on the spot—two runs and then a take.
>
> Q: Read it immediately?
>
> That's why they're paying you more, and that's why you are known as a soloist in the business; that's why you're in demand. And we better do it. So those times, like I say, two per cent of the time . . . you get 'em.
>
> Q: So you have to come up with it?
>
> Yes. Then it gets pretty critical, everyone is nervous, a lot is at stake, but those moments are rare, just here and there . . . a couple of weeks, then you have to use every bit of talent and tricks and whatever learning your past experience has taught you. The rest of the time you come and sit down . . . nothing. Many sessions I come there and read a book, the leaders don't know it, you know . . . or I'm in a trance, far away, and I play the job and don't even know I'm there or what I'm playing.
>
> Q: You only use your skills and talents to their fullest only at times?
>
> Yes. Most of the things we do are very routine. They're supposed to be, I guess.

A brass player's feelings about this were almost identical.

> Sometimes you have to stretch, sometimes you don't. You know for some calls you just sit there and play dumb things, simple tunes, half notes. God, what a drag. Then the next thing you know you'll be into some acrobatics like playing

very high parts for a couple of hours and in this situation everyone's talent is on the line and we're all on the hot seat.

A viola player summed up his feelings about musical challenge in the studios by pointing to the type of notes he usually played:

Are there areas where the music is usually dull? Let me tell you how dull it can be. We did some real B horror pictures some years ago at the studio . . . very, very dull. There was one where the strings played harmonics, sustained harmonics, well, about 150 bars of the same note. Nothing, absolutely nothing but footballs, whole notes. The guys in the section, we were all dying to play a half note. It was hard to remember where you were, to keep your place, with 150 bars of one note and nothing different.

These particular performers are more opinionated and dramatic than most; their views, however, occur with surprising frequency among these musicians. The majority of those interviewed felt that studio work did not use their skills and talents to their fullest advantage, or if so, only at certain times.[2] A smaller proportion, the string instrumentalists especially, felt that this work did not tap their highest musical potential.

A violin player spoke for many of his colleagues when he expressed his dissatisfaction with studio work. He was explicit in comparing his present work to his extensive training and emphasized his need for creative playing. He bitterly discussed his work from this standpoint.

I don't know if this occurs any more to the hardened commercial player, "Well, it's just a job." You play, it's dull, and you get the hell out. You're just doing a job. Of course there are what I would call the more sensitive players who have been trained, brought up with a well-rounded education and have played in conservatories, and have enjoyed prominence

2. Percentage distributions of responses to "Does playing in the commercial field use your skills and talents to their fullest advantage?": String players, yes–8, no–92; woodwind, reeds, and French horn players, yes–48, no–52; brass, sax, and percussion players, yes–40, no–69.

as soloists. They have had exhaustive training in chamber music, have learned to love the great literature and want to be continually reminded, and remind themselves of great music. So here they are sitting on the recording stage recording and playing some of the trash they have to do in the service of a story that is sheer claptrap. As they watch it on the screen, they must certainly have in mind the prostituting effects of this on their art, their skills, on their craft.

As noted in Chapter 3 string players, particularly violin, viola, and cello instrumentalists, often aspired to be either soloists or play in chamber ensembles. These players tend to view the demands placed upon their skills by free-lance commercial work as relatively low in comparison to those made by concert work. An additional source of monotony, already noted above, is the type of music, usually written for strings. The following three statements by string players illustrate this point:

> Most of this work uses about 20 per cent of your ability. Once in a while you'll find a composer who's trying something, and you have to use quite a bit of skill; otherwise the only thing is doing it accurately and carefully. You know, it's hardly work.
>
> We're just a cog in a wheel, it's a mechanical job, except for certain conductors and certain composers—they make more of an artistic venture out of it.
>
> You never use the equipment you've been trained to use, most of this crap for the strings is just half notes, footballs. But then again, a composer might write a wild piece of music and you might get a solo to play; then it's fun. So sometimes you're on the hot seat and sometimes you're not.

Thus, the contrast between training, musical aspirations, and background and the fluctuations from difficult to easy work demands introduced by the nature of film composition and, in particular, the fluctuations in various studio calls, appear to increase the felt monotony that comes from unchallenging work. Moreover, the actual work role of the string instrumentalist reinforces this feeling. Since he works largely within an organized string section, the string player must blend with the other players in his section, who are playing the same or similar notes as he. In contrast, most non-string players are in a sense soloists, in that many passages played with the orchestra are individual parts and audible to all. These factors lead to an anonymous place in the work process, except for those string players who are principals of sections and who are in a position to play solo and exposed parts if and when they occur. One string player, who sits in the middle of a studio orchestra, said: "As a violinist you're working in a section, and you're part of a group. You have to become integrated. If you have any ideas, you just keep quiet, unless you're the concertmaster." From the viewpoint of the string player, studio work seldom calls for the use of present capacities or skills developed over the years of training; it is largely routine with occasional moments of challenge. Such moments depend on what the particular composer writes, where the musician is sitting in the string section, the difficulty of his part, etc.

Although the majority of woodwind, brass, percussion, and other non-string players also reported that commercial work did not take full advantage of their skills, more of these musicians than of the string players tended to emphasize the positive and often challenging aspects of their studio jobs. Again, the talent and ingenuity of the composer provided opportunities to use their technical abilities, solve musical problems (in their parts, for example), exercise independent initiative, and "really get a chance to play."

Paradoxically, the most demanding music is often the most poorly composed. One frequently mentioned challenge for these players was mastering "unplayable" music. A favorite anecdote was of the composer who does not know the range, flexibility, or sonority of an instrument, or who writes the wrong music for the wrong instrument. It was clear that the musician could perform the part, but such contingencies often create tension-filled moments.

> Every once in a while I'll run into a situation where somebody who is not that skillful a writer will write for the entire orchestra things that are unplayable on a given horn. You don't know what you're going to get; like, one morning you might have a jazz call, a hard jazz call, with F's and G's. So O.K., you play it. And then the guy (the composer) might turn around and start writing skips and all kinds of things like that that are just damn near unplayable, or go beyond your capacity to play.

Here is a reed player in his forties who carefully differentiated between what composers write and what they want, and some of the fears this contingency creates for him.

> Does it use my skills and talent? Well, the demands can be very difficult. Some composers don't even know what they're writing so you have to be flexible, be ready for anything, and be able to get around the problem. And frequently the composer doesn't know what he wants and so if you can't play this impossible set of notes, well, he can find another flute or clarinet player and simply not ask for you. It doesn't matter how hard it is, if you don't make it, you'll find yourself out with that composer, even though the part would sound better and probably be played better by another instrument like a bassoon. So to answer your question, sometimes you have to play over your head, sometimes you really have to stretch; most of the time it's critical.

These musicians face the additional work problems of flexibility, stamina, and endurance. Because of the physical demands on the embouchures as well as on the body, one test of their skills is the ability to play long and demanding calls, or a series of free-lance calls in one day or throughout the week. The dilemma of challenging and monotonous calls was expressed, in several cases, as an unexpected trap and therefore a test of the player's mental skills and physical condition. A brass player related one particularly grinding studio call.

Q: Does your work in commercial music use your skills and talents to their fullest advantage?

Yes and I'll tell you why, it's because this business is a trap. There are times, visual situations in films that require, or make it possible for a composer to really write something of substance, and there it is—right in front of you. If the product is good and the producer-director has taste and gets a good composer who spends his time writing quality music, then you're going to be challenged. And if you've let yourself fall into the trap of anticipating those nothing scores, and you let your playing drop, you have this challenge, and the moment of truth arrives, and you can fall all over yourself. If you do, it can mean the end of you. You've got to keep your skills up.

Q: That would be a challenge.

Right. If you run through a period of, say, a couple of months where you haven't really played a challenging score for you, you might find yourself on a six- or eight-hour call the next day. I remember one day we were doing two or three shows, five or six tapes on each one with the main title and the end title, the playons and playouts, and all the music was very high, high E's and all that, time and time again, and playing as hard as you can. Well, we were begging for mercy after four hours of this.

Q: These types of calls vary, don't they?

That's just it. You go eight hours of solid playing one day and your lips are like sausages and the next day maybe you're off, or you'll work two days and then you'll just do dull stuff for weeks.

Since these musicians seldom know how difficult a call will be, the pace at which they work often leads to strain on their lips, and it is therefore no surprise that these musicians, in contrast to their string-playing colleagues, complain of working too fast and of the pressure that this puts on their abilities. The phrase "there's no room for error" captures the psychological and physical strain, which may be more intense for particular instrumentalists because of the nature of their instruments. The differences between the responses of the wind and string players suggest that, although the extent to which any musician's skills will be utilized depends upon the composer, the work loads on string players are generally easier because past skills are usually adequate to cope with studio writing, while wind players more frequently face challenges to their technique when calls are physically demanding or when many of their work calls come at once.

Unlike their string-playing colleagues, wind and percussion players with big-band and jazz backgrounds emphasize that their career moves into commercial studio work led to an upgrading of their previous skills. Even though they feel that a good deal of their studio work does not tap the full potential of their skills, these particular musicians usually emphasize the more difficult or challenging calls in describing their work. Moreover, possible disjunctions between past experience and present skill levels are played down. If work fluctuates between routine and crisis calls, musicians playing particular instruments — brass, saxophones, clarinets, etc. — typically emphasize the demands of pressure in the studios, and find a source of pride in dealing with such contingencies. In contrast to string players, there is a definite tendency for these players — particularly brass, saxophones, and percussion — to have preferred commercial work for intrinsic reasons and, once in this setting, to report that their skills and talents are used to their fullest. Past skills and present work roles influence one another in this case. A clear example of the differences between the string players and others can be found in the following two interviews. First, a percussionist describes his rewards:

Q: Did playing in commercial music in the stuio setting disillusion you in any way?

No, I don't think so. I was suddenly thrown into this tremendous competition out here, playing with musicians way over my head and playing music that was extremely challenging and I didn't have the kind of training . . . . Well, I was suddenly aware of all kinds of things about the music and of ways to approach the instrument that I just hadn't thought about before. Nobody had explained anything to me, I'd never seen it done. It was a constant test. Achieving that level of playing with those people was something.

Q: It was challenging then?

Sure, and it was very invigorating, it still is — sometimes. Now times you can just get sick and tired of it and think "Oh, what time is it? Are we through yet?" But some days the music is beautiful and it's a ball to do it. You've got to be ready for everything.

Compare this with the following statement by a violin player with conservatory training and with a past career in some of the major symphonies in this country:

Q: Did playing commercial music in the studio setting disillusion you in any way?

No, there's nothing to be disillusioned about; that presuposses an illusion and I had no illusions about this business. Disenchantment is a better term, but then there would have to be enchantment in the first place and there wasn't. I've done a lot of playing of chamber music for fun over the years; I had too much playing of good music to feel that commercial work had very much to offer me in terms of musical satisfaction.

Q: How about the demands on your skills?

In any case, the demands are so low that I could actually never practice and keep working in the business for the rest of my life.

Q: Why is that?

Why? Well, I remember when I was just breaking in, what they would write for the strings, first there were pages and pages of long whole notes, then maybe a little run. It really hasn't improved. Strings are just the frosting on the cake to the producers and others, they just add them on. Also, I might mention that most commercial leaders came from a pop field, their backgrounds are in pop and that's it. They really don't write for strings at all.

Dignity and Its Discontents

There are two major components to the concept of "dignity" expressed by these musicians. First, all of the respondents displayed pride in themselves as instrumentalists, based on what we might call traditional artistic norms. Second, because of their training and early commitment, plus their career success, these musicians tend to express a specific occupational identity: they regard themselves as "musicians" rather than as "studio or free-lance players." Their pride in themselves as competent performers is deep and pervasive.

Such dignity has its drawbacks; these are most clearly reflected in the musicians' resentment of music and studio situations which do not affirm their identities as talented performers. In the deepest sense, this disjunction is between the performer and the industry: it stems from the unique combination of a highly skilled group of musicians, with their own standards which define excellence in work, performing in an elaborate production setting in which music is subject to extreme rationalization and subdivision.

Here are several excerpts from the interviews which deal with personal pride. The respondent was asked if he had to "play his best all the time" in his studio work, and the similarities in language used to answer this question are surprising. One elder statesman, when asked, peered back at me for a few seconds, then said with no uncertain personal dignity:

> I believe it is necessary to play commercial music, no matter how poor, no matter how poorly written, or how poorly starved a film score is for good ideas, I feel that for my own private pride of performance, it deserves the best I can give it. I never compromise on that.

A young brass player expressed the values of personal musicianship in more numerical terms when he said:

> I always give 100 per cent, even if it's only two measures of a whole note. I try to produce 100 per cent of quality on the simplest music. It has nothing to do with how difficult the music is, it's the only way I know how to play.

This last phrase is found throughout the interviews and reflects the years of commitment and energy these performers have devoted to perfecting their skills. The strong sense of personal satisfaction that comes from realizing self-set standards of excellence was emphasized by a cellist when asked what he liked best about being a free-lance musician. He paused, then said:

> Of course you convince yourself that all it is is money, but the personal satisfaction is also there. Have you seen us work? You watch it. Whenever a musician has a cue to play, when he's exposed, he's playing his best. At the utmost, that's it, no matter what it is. It all goes back to your own standards, standards you set for yourself when you play an instrument.

A woodwind player who has been in the studios since the contract orchestras stressed a similar theme when he explained his concern with quality performance under any conditions. He seemed upset when asked if he had to play his best all the time:

> What do you mean have to? *I* require me to play the best I can at all times. I don't care what it requires, I'm not interested in that. I require me to play the best for my own

self-satisfaction. I try to play beautifully whatever I'm doing, for my own pride.

What we see here is more than pride in technical competence or in the accomplishment of an individual job. It is the dignity that comes from both attempting to achieve and to maintain personal standards of musicianship. It should be noted that most of the players indicated they had to play their best all the time, and that these personal ideals and standards were the primary reasons underlying this response.[3]

The most direct impact of self-dignity is seen in their attitudes towards the individual jobs they do in the studios. There is a feeling that a musician should never let his skills slip, regardless of what he is called upon to play. Although a majority of respondents report that commercial work rarely or never uses their skills to their *fullest* advantage, a much larger proportion indicates that they have to *play their best* all the time. There are higher ideals than efficient performance of motion picture, television film, rock and roll music, and jingles. A clarinet player explained that pride in one's musicianship was, indeed, often difficult — especially when there were long stretches of uninteresting music to play:

> If you look down your nose as a matter of course at this music you have to play and conclude it's *always* like that, then very likely there may be a negative effect on your playing ability. You know . . . this obsolete junk you see before your eyes, it's musical nonsense.

He continued:

> But if you have self-respect, a sense of personality, you want to always deliver the goods, no matter what the occasion, it's personal integrity.

3. Percentage distributions of responses to "Do you have to play your best all the time?": String players, yes-70, no-30; woodwind, reeds, and French horn players, yes-76, no-24; brass, sax, and percussion players, yes-88, no-12.

Having looked at the pervasiveness of integrity and self-dignity, the deep dissatisfaction with the work problems created by the demands of the production process becomes easier to understand. The structure of work and its impact on personal experience in commercial studios is an example of the conflict between efficiency and human values.[4] In general, these musicians expressed resentment of studio efficiency when it imposed on their musical values and dignity. Undertones of resignation and bitterness were expressed by one of the busiest percussionists in town:

> There are calls where you have to sacrifice certain musical values . . . values you've set for yourself, and at times you sacrifice a lot more than necessary.
>
> Q: Why is that? Could you give me an example?
>
> Well, there's time. You've not given time to play it musically, to get *into* it, to play it musically. I think this is the thing that bugs us most. The music is bad, the mixers are lousy, you play beautifully and the play-back it sounds terrible and they say, "Take it!" You say to yourself, "OK, if that's the way they want it, to hell with 'em, if *they* don't care *I* sure as hell won't."

A brass player relished the opportunity to tell me about some of the work conditions he finds especially degrading. Like his colleague above, his solution is to give them what they want and to forget about it.

> Some studios are so cheap, they'll do anything to save a buck. You know, rush, rush . . . "Come on guys, let's get this done," and all that. So you go in, the film starts, the clicks start, and they take everything—mistakes and all. Some people want you to come in, play it, and get the hell out. They can't be bothered with doing it musically. But in this case, hell, just grind it out, go home, have a few belts and forget it.

A cellist expressed his disdain with the treatment music

4. Daniel Bell, "Work and Its Discontents," *The End of Ideology* (New York: Collier Books, 1961), pp. 227–271.

receives on certain TV film calls and the negative consequences of this for the integrity of the performers, the composer, and conductor:

> Everything is done with a budget in mind. Unfortunately in some television film much of the time, you'll do two takes and there might be a goof or sloppy entrance, or intonation problems. So the conductor or someone else will say, "Let's hear it back." And they'll hear it back and the mistakes are there and they'll say "let's hear it back with the dialogue." And they'll say it's good enough. As far as I'm concerned it's lousy. And the standard answer for that is that it's good enough for a three-inch TV speaker in someone's home. "Who will ever hear it?" So there you are, the head of the music department saying "fine, fine, print it — smack." That's frustrating, there's nothing worse than a schlock outfit. We'd like to get it right, perfect, that's the way we think. The composer wants to get it right, he wrote the thing. But we don't have ten more minutes to get it right because of the budget and all that. So in view of it . . . the cue's ok, so, you go on to the next take.

Production personnel create conditions under which music, and the studio musician, are treated as secondary and often meaningless elements in film-making. It is ironic that the film and recording business goes to considerable effort to obtain a highly select and talented group of artists, requires them to be equipped to perform any type of music, and then, because of the nature of the medium often downgrades their labor and its products. These musicians, as well as brass players working in rock and roll settings, expressed much chagrin at the fact that in those instances where numerous takes are recorded and much fuss is made over the quality of instrumental sound, often their sound on the completed record is barely audible, or hidden under other instruments and voices. In this case they have no control over the final disposition of the recorded performance which may be spliced, edited, and altered in terms of orchestral balance and to better fit under the dialogue.

Time and budgets are routine problems. timing is also a persistent pressure; this is best illustrated by looking at how the requirements of synchronization often undermine a performer's flexible interpretation of his part, make it hard to sustain the musical inertia of rhythm (or get into the rhythmic groove), and demand a coldness of playing. A young player discussed the impact of click tracks on his view of most film work and the context in which cool efficiency was a virtue.

> You go on a film date and things don't go smoothly and after twelve takes of the same thing, the emotion is gone, the best you can do is get the notes. You don't take a chance to be emotional when you're doing this music. If you try to phrase and get the most out of it you might mess up a take. You get the clicks banging away in the ear and you can't make mistakes because it's dangerous. After all, they just want sound effects, they don't want music — you're just a mechanical unit, like a sound technician.

At the same time, however, there are several ways in which the musicians can neutralize or minimize the dominance of recording technology in their work. First, they work in various studios which use varying kinds of synchronizing devices. On one call, the recording session can be totally mechanized by the use of click tracks; on the next, the conductor may follow only a timing clock, thereby leaving the musicians free to follow him. Some calls will shift back and forth between these methods. In other words, how synchronization will be effected depends on studio production policies and conductor preferences and is thus a variable work contingency. A second and related factor is that the skill of the conductor can also lessen the influence of technology on the performers. The better conductors are adept in studio work and are able to ex-

plain to the orchestra the effects that are needed and how
the music is to be performed. The musicians can follow
them with more confidence, thus making the use of synchronizing devices less obtrusive. Third, the most important, the musicians tend not to be overwhelmed by the
technology that surrounds them because, even in that
setting, they are called upon to exercise considerable judgment in playing various styles of music, solving technical
problems on their instrument, and being prepared for the
uncertainty of any call. Although at times they see themselves as just "a mechanical unit, like a sound technician,"
the use made of their skills and talents in dealing with
these aspects of their work allows them to find satisfactions above and beyond merely playing routine and dull
scores.

Although the commercial musician can thus be free
from direct technological pressure under certain conditions, these diverse work settings, conductors, and production pressures *can* intensify the more "alienating" tendencies of studio technology and work organization. Several factors contribute to this: the studio's or independent
producer's policy towards music, costs of the individual
film or record, and the music itself. As I have noted, some
studios—because of production, monetary, or personnel
problems—relegate the music to a very minor place. And
if music is used, they can schedule heavy work loads (too
few hours in which to record). From the musicians' personal perspective, such situations exemplify the special
deprivations and sense of powerlessness which come from
having little control over the time and quality of their
performances. This industry-wide downgrading of a performer's importance was mentioned by our respondents as
one of the most negative features of commercial studio
work. A genuine sense of pride and satisfaction comes
from working with composers and conductors, and with

studio personnel, who realize the importance of careful scoring and meticulous recording. In these situations, the musician's competence is affirmed rather than undermined, as one young percussion player indicated when he contrasted types of composers and conductors, and made some comments on the career pressures they face:

Q: How important is music to the total production in pictures?

Take X for example. He has the producers and directors sold on the use of music and doing a call for him is beautiful, you love him. His music is on a very high level, it's demanding, he treats you right, so you treat him the same way and that's a joy. But we have too many composers and conductors in this business who will do anything, *anything,* to work. So they sell their music as a cheap commodity and they sell *you* as a cheap commodity — I resent that very much. They put it on the level of a guy delivering newspapers or something like that, there's quite a bit of difference — right?

Q: Right. Any difference in motion pictures and television film?

Now in television film, very rarely do you work with someone who is trying to do something really worthwhile, and again that's an individual thing with the composer. Some composers, everything . . . well, no matter what it is, it's important to them. Just because it's a short TV show doesn't make it any less to him. And these are the kind of people you really like and respect. Working with these people . . . this is great, because that's the way I feel about music, and I resent the other people who cheapen it as a product and cheapen it in every way. Some of these guys are so incredibly bad, to my way of thinking, it's just junk . . . really, just junk.

Composers, conductors, and sound technicians play a crucial role in mediating the perceived problems of film work, for they determine the quality of music written and recorded, and the atmosphere of the sessions themselves. From these players' perspective, the arbiter of what is a good take and a quality performance should be someone who is knowledgable and concerned about what happens to the music. Thus, it is understandable that, when describing the misuse of their talents, they direct their most severe criticisms towards those who fail to live up to these standards, bend too easily under budget pressures, and downgrade the musician.

Tempering these negative attitudes towards the people surrounding them, however, is the feeling that "we're all in the same boat": that all of the creating and performing artists involved in the recording of free-lance calls are subject to the frustrations resulting from the place of music in the production process and the often unequal power relations between the music department and other production units.

But if pride in skills is often undermined by the impositions of technology, policies, and sometimes incompetence of others, the variety and unpredictability inherent in free-lance employment lead to a strong sense of technical expertise — the ability to perform successfully any type of music under any studio condition. These musicians tend to shift attention away from the less interesting, or degrading, uses to which their skills are put and to emphasize those times when they have to go all out. They balance the marked negative feelings about certain studio situations, composers, and conductors with positive statements about their more challenging or demanding experiences. The musicians are quick to point out the range of possibilities within which their skills are utilized, as well as the expertise it takes to handle "anything they throw at us," i.e., the difficulty of the music, personal idiosyncrasies of conductors, time pressure, and other contingencies. We might ask: Is this merely an effort to play up the more demanding calls, thereby playing down the dissatisfactions which accompany unchallenging work? What is the specific content of a commercial musician's pride in work?

Howard Becker has pointed out that musicians who

"go commercial" adjust to this type of work by adopting what he calls a craftsmanship orientation. For the jazz players which he discusses, the shift is presumably away from the "higher" goals of artistic freedom and creativity and towards technical virtuosity. The musician who adopts this view of work and himself ". . . no longer concerns himself with the *kind* of music he plays. Instead, he is interested only in whether it is played *correctly,* in whether he has the skills necessary to do the job the way it ought to be done. He finds his pride and self-respect in being able to 'cut' any kind of music, in always giving an adequate performance."[5]

The musician's pride in technical expertise varies with the work setting in which he performs. Becker gives the following examples: "The man who works in bars with small groups will pride himself on knowing hundreds (or even thousands) of songs and being able to play them in any key . . . . The man who works in a night club or radio studio boasts of his ability to read any kind of music accurately and precisely at sight."[6] Similarly musicians in film and phonograph record work emphasize that quickness and accuracy are essential skills in a setting where time is valuable and recording costs enormous. However, unlike work in pit orchestras, nightclubs, or even radio and television networks, the work of musicians in the film industry consists of a number of different jobs in different studios. Variety is an inevitable aspect of studio work, since each film requires new music; and the musician constantly faces different composers, conductors, working conditions, and sets of colleagues on the various calls he accepts.

Like some of the musicians interviewed by Becker, these players take pride in their abilities to perform

5. Howard Becker, *Outsiders* (New York: Free Press, 1963), pp. 112–113.

6. Becker, *op. cit.,* p. 113.

efficiently in the recording setting. Although most reported that commercial music did not use their skills and
talents to their fullest advantage all the time, film work is
seen as particularly demanding because of the speed of
the work process. Several used language almost identical
to this in describing their work and their abilities:

You have to figure out what the job requires and do it quickly. You get a genuine sense of pride out of being so clever
and flexible that you can play in any style, right there . . . play
it through once, know what the conductor wants, and then
play it the second time for a polished take.

Aside from playing accurately, a musician is required to
exercise initiative in determining what the composers and
conductors want, even if they are unclear in their instructions, or unrealistically demanding in the music they
write. Free-lancers see themselves as often saving conductors from mistakes made on the podium. Timing and
time pressure were discussed at length by a young brass
player.

You have to be able to understand what the composer wants.
First of all, the composer who might be the conductor gets on
the podium, we'll say for a TV film. The film has already been
shot, and edited, and the producer sits down with the composer, and they roll the film, and they discuss where they
need the music. Now this can be one Friday. And the composer has to be ready to record on Monday. That means he
sits up for 48 to 72 hours writing frantically, getting it done,
cranking out the copies so it will be ready for scoring. Very
often, when we're doing the first cue, the second half of the
show is still being copied.
Q: So he's on the podium ready to go . . .
. . . by that time he's a nervous wreck. And he has to have the
feeling that the guys are with him. If they're against him, he
gets very insecure. The guys have to understand his language.
They have to understand his personality and when he says
something—the guys have to understand. They have to project themselves into his particular mind and figure out what

he really means. Sometimes with copying errors, we're actually trying to save time by working out the problem ourselves to get the notes right. So he sees us talking and he gets mad, these things happen and there's a fine balance involved here trying to help the conductor. Now we have very talented and experienced conductors and things go comparably easier. Sometimes you have a talented composer and a less talented conductor, so we try to make up for his [the conductor's] lacks.

Another player sees the superior talents of the free-lancer as salvaging the mistakes and failures of composers. He put it rather bluntly:

It's our job to make junk sound good. We make these guys look good.

As specialists in versatility, studio players often compare themselves with symphony orchestra or big-band players. Two composer-conductors interviewed made similar comments about the speed, accuracy, and coolness of these musicians:

Some, not all, symphony players are simply not geared to the quick thinking required. They have sightreading problems for one thing. It's not necessary for them to play it right for the first time, the first take. They hear it, get soaked in the general atmosphere for one or two weeks before a performance. In the studio, the conductor wants you to play it fairly accurately the first time so he can hear it, hear what it is, and then make the take.

I've worked in Nashville, the big bands, and all around, and I'd say for sheer ability and speed the greatest musicians are out here in Los Angeles. They're unbelievably fast . . . play anything, they learn anything fast, they aren't rigid, you know, classical . . . .

Being versatile means not only knowing what the conductor wants and being able to play it, but it also implies an ability to bend, to change styles of playing, and even to change the tone produced on an instrument from one take or call to the next. A saxophone-reed doubler, like many

other of his colleagues, contrasted himself to some legitimate orchestra musicians:

> There are types of guys ... many reed players don't bend,
> they're not flexible. Some don't even get the right sound in
> the studio or they refuse to play different. So [a composer]
> wants a light, French sound on the oboe for example and
> [another composer] prefers a dark, fat, German sound and
> you have to bend, to be able to play them all.

Using recent studio calls as examples, the following
players made these invidious comparisons between themselves and others:

> I did a picture with X and he said he wanted me because
> what he wrote called for a certain line played without any
> vibrato and I know some of the legit players would never
> think of playing anything without vibrato. He said "try not to
> use vibrato, playing with a dead sound, you know, try to
> sound like Miles [Davis]."

> I doubt whether symphony players or other guys really have
> all the things down, all the experience that comes with know-
> ing every style, of having gone through the mill ... I have to
> be funny, be a clown, be serious, play jazz, there's all types of
> music and all types of challenges. You have to improvise, the
> composer will even tell you to do anything you want
> ... blow.

> You're pounding on high notes like we were last week for a
> couple of hours and all your blood is gone out of your lips and
> then they have you turn right around and play something soft
> and delicate, in the upper register, or play a little jazz, or a
> bugle call with finesse. Not many guys can make it come
> off....

With few exceptions, the musicians contend that flexibility is as essential to studio performing as speed, accuracy, endurance, and intonation. It is basic to the jobs
they are called upon to perform. Thus, the ability to
handle a variety of musical styles and to be prepared for
any contingency that may arise or any demand that may
be made upon their musical and technical skills is a source

of work satisfaction and pride. Free-lance work strengthens the musicians' pride in their expertise, specifically when they are called upon to solve problems which may develop in the course of a work call. These players are concerned with competence, and, unlike the casual dance musicians interviewed by Becker, they are concerned with the kind of music they play, who has written it, and who conducts it.

It is a mistake to view music which is dull and routine, and therefore unchallenging to the player's skills, as simply an inescapable and generalized condition of studio work. Demands fluctuate, and satisfaction depends on the musician's specific work calls. In summary, two points deserve mention. First, among these musicians one finds many who are clearly dissatisfied with the uses to which their talents are put. String players more than others express marked negative feelings about their calls, often stressing the disjunctions between their skill level (and their personal artistic horizons) and present work. They see much of what they do as unchallenging, routine, and degrading. Second, the negative aspects of commercial jobs are felt more intensely by players who are not as favorably situated on the informal career ladder in Hollywood. Status in the occupational hiring system has obvious consequences on the type and quality of work a player will be called upon to do. Musicians less in demand (not in the inner fraternity) are not likely to be hired for the "better" calls — those with more interesting music, better conductors, and challenging work. But even musicians in the inner circle do not succeed in escaping entirely from "bad calls," "dumb jobs," or a lack of "real music" to play.

Judged by the standards of craftsmanship in the writings of Mills, Marx, Veblen, Tilgher, and others, the studio musicians are paradoxical. They bring to this setting high standards of work performance. They are the interpreters of previously composed works and do not shape a work from conception to execution. Unlike the model of the individual artisan, their work is done in highly collective settings. They do not have the protection of powerful guild or union. They do not have complete control over the amount of work they do. While they do have total mastery over the sound which they produce, the pacing of music is often predetermined and the production goals of the studio often override individual standards of quality performance. They can not determine what music they will play (except by turning down a studio call), how rationalized the pacing will be, the amount of studio time spent on recording takes, the quality of overall sound reproduction, or the final disposition of their taped performance on film or phonograph recordings. These technical operations are done by others.

While these contingencies tend to downgrade the musician's pride in his work, they are by no means consistent in their effects. Each call (whether in motion pictures, television, rock and roll, or commercial jingles) is unique, and this inhibits the complete rationalization of work and downgrading of skills often found in bureaucratic and machine-work organizations where the product and work task are standardized, repetitive, and unchanging. With variable demands, musicians are faced with routine and crisis situations, challenging and prosaic jobs, and talented as well as incompetent composers, conductors, and technicians.

CHAPTER SIX

The Hiring Structure and
Status Situation

While the successful handling of studio work contingencies allows the free-lance musician opportunities to acquire and retain valuables, his commitment is also linked to the power and prestige that he enjoys. Considerable tension and intrigue center around reducing those aspects of the occupational scene which threaten his personal sense of dignity, exercising control over the hiring procedures, getting a step ahead of colleague competitors, and escaping from studio dirty work.

In tracing successful career lines into the inner circle, Chapter 4 emphasized the importance of attracting the attention of colleagues, building a reputation, and in general, reducing the hazards of a career. It was noted that whatever job security a musician has is directly tied to how many contractors, composers, or leaders call him and request his services. This creates a major source of unpredictability for the musician over and above the recurrent variations in studio productions, type of orchestration

used, and various fads and fashions in the music composed for films, TV, records, and commercial transcriptions. In the lopsided power relationships with contractors, for example, being in demand by various hiring
agents makes possible a sense of control over the conditions of work and of satisfaction at being selected. Building accounts with contractors constitutes a major investment of time and effort; the accounts are not relin-
quished easily, and they enhance the musician's commitment to the studio scene. But only continuing effort
can sustain these connections. As these musicians report,
they are only as good as their last call, only as secure as
the number of people who like their playing. Predictably,
70 per cent of those interviewed said they had little or no
job security. This is all the more important in the light of
many empirical studies which emphasize that security and
regularity of employment is a significant factor in job
satisfaction and commitment.[1]

Let me quote some representative material and describe the following themes: (1) the basic perspective and
consensus centering around control over the conditions of
studio hiring, (2) free-lancers' views of contractors and the
power game, (3) the importance of building accounts and
of securing some measure of independence, and (4) performers' sensitivity to colleague standards and controls.

A player who is on the lists of the two most powerful
contractors in Hollywood was sarcastic about his vulnerability to their evaluations, but at the same time he emphasized some of the strategies in picking calls and being

1. These studies are reviewed in Frederick Herzberg et al., *Job
Attitudes: Review of Research and Opinion* (Pittsburgh: Pittsburgh
Psychological Service, 1957); Robert Blauner, "Work Satisfaction and
Industrial Trends in Modern Society," in R. Bendix and S. M. Lipset
(eds.), *Class, Status, and Power* (New York: Free Press of Glencoe,
1966), pp. 473–487; E. A. Friedmann and R. J. Havighurst, *The
Meaning of Work and Retirement* (Chicago: University of Chicago
Press, 1954).

independent. The following is in response to a question asked each musician: what did they like best about being a free-lance performer?

> The most obvious thing is that it pays very well. It's the only kind of music which does pay. I don't feel at all that I'm part of a great industry, 'cause I'm not. It's a lousy industry. As I say, many of the composers are so mediocre, and the contractors are morons, just nothing. It's very rare when a contractor knows something. You could almost say that a prerequisite for becoming a contractor who'll become all-powerful is that they [sic] were such mediocre musicians themselves that they never made it as players. So they more or less have the power of life and death over you. Either they hire you or they don't. Right now I find that I am loyal to certain contractors who hire me for all their work. So I try to keep myself available for them. But for some others, I couldn't care less whether they call me or they don't. I'm trying to be as independent as possible in a business which really has very little security. This allows me to turn down work that I don't want to do.

A most impressive feature of this musician's view, as well as of those of a majority of the others, was the extreme saliency and emotional intensity of their attitudes towards contractor's power. If power is the ability to get others to do one's will, then studio contractors, from the outlook of our respondents, exercise a great deal of it. Over 80 per cent of these players expressed resentment at either the absolute control that contractors have over their career fate and their yearly earnings, or at the questionable talents of contractors as hiring agents.

An established string player was very touchy about contractors who fail to call the musicians specifically requested by composers and leaders. This to him was an unfair use of power in the service of some other game the hiring agent was playing. His language is representative of the respondents.

> One big problem is that the contractors have too much power

over the life of the musician. No one should have that much power. Sometimes, a composer asks for you especially for one of his calls. A contractor, and I know several instances where this has happened to me, will not use you or he may use you for one call and then not for another. It's very bad. The real problem is that your money comes from the contractor.

Here is an opinionated reed player who clearly indicated his esteem for contractors:

These guys [contractors] like to play games, you know, you're gone for a few weeks and you're not available for their calls and before you know it someone else is on the list and has taken your place. They're frustrated musicians anyway, they don't know anything about music; really, they can't recognize talent. They're just clerks, glorified secretaries. They shouldn't have the power they do. You stand a chance of losing a quarter or half the income for a year if a big contractor, like X, becomes cool to you.

This aspect of the work situation threatens the performers because their sense of control over their fate is diminished by the amount of power held by studio contractors. The following player, a man of strong opinions, had a good idea of his worth. There was no false modesty when he stressed intrigues with contractors:

You always have to be at their obeisance. That's a pressure. They operate to me like pint-sized dictators, like Jehovah. Your destiny is in the hands of someone else, in the hands of a leader or contractor. It's determined by a telephone. This is my pet gripe with the business. You're at the mercy of a guy calling you or not.

One brass player stressed the problems which free-lance hiring poses for the musician, who, caught between contractors and sponsors, and the status hierarchy implied by the contractor's call list, ends up experiencing a sense of confusion and even resentment.

You're on a contractor's list and you can be removed from it in a minute. There's no security whatsoever in this game.

Your reputation is on paper, on the contractor's list. Your worth is only to the few people you work for. It takes breaks, luck, and the proper people pushing you. Nobody really likes it . . . you depend on phone calls for your living. I really think most of us end up feeling like pawns on a chessboard after a while, you know, pushed around by contractors who are competing with each other, everyone trying to get the big names . . . it's wild.

Ideally, hiring contingencies should be settled by contractors and musicians reaching open agreements about when the players will be called, their positions on the lists, and the amount of loyalty to be exchanged for work calls. However, these procedures are never made fully explicit. For one thing, the uncertainties of calls loom too large; second, the contractor could weaken his bargaining power by letting all this information out; and third, like good poker players, musicians in demand prefer to negotiate and bargain with strong hands. The information screen between musicians and contractors, of course, favors those in demand; they are in preferred positions. It hurts those further down on the contractors' lists. The musicians' language reflects their relative powerlessness: they stress their economic dependence on contractors, the impersonal power of the telephone, the perception of the "big names" in demand. All of these factors increase their frustration with hiring practices. A string player who had the best sense of humor of all the respondents jokingly compared free-lancing to another "profession."

I sit home and wait for the phone to ring. When I'm called, I go and play. I compare my business to that of a prostitute. I'm a callman, you see. I go where I'm called and I get paid. There's no emotional involvement there. It's very convenient. I perform my duties to the best of my abilities and I don't get involved.

If the power of contractors over musicians is one source of job dissatisfaction, the musicians are under no formal, contractual obligation to accept a contractor's jobs. Their free-lance reputations allow them to spread their accounts, plus the opportunity to turn down calls. This gives them some countervailing power from their inherently subordinate position on the labor market. As several musicians expressed it, "The main advantage for us is independence; it's much better than contracts." This independence presumably allows them flexibility in arranging their work schedules and gives them a chance to choose "good" rather than "bad" calls. One busy percussionist, when asked whether there were any jobs that were dull and monotonous in free-lance work, said:

> I don't do that type of work, or try not to do it. I'm busy enough to have a choice about the kind of work I'll do. Without the contractors and others knowing it you can say, "I'm busy that day." It's good, they have a choice and they want you and you also have a choice. This sort of puts us both in the same position.

Once secured, a good bargaining position makes possible a sense of freedom, pride, and satisfaction. It constitutes a valuable difficult to relinquish and therefore is a basis for occupational commitment.

> Q: What do you like most about being a free-lance player?
> I'm my own boss. You know it's like this: if I decided to turn a contractor down, I can, I'm not obligated to anyone, there are no contracts. Believe me, there are some conductors and contractors I've turned down just because I don't care to work with them. Even though it's a loss of money, I feel musically that . . . well, some of these people offend me, particularly in the way they handle the orchestra. I did this as late as last week. I turned down a call and did nothing all day. That was a loss of six hours. I don't tell other people I did it; I just say I'm busy on another date.

The free-lancer, as these respondents suggest, achieves a strong bargaining position and increased flexibility in the scheduling of work calls. Consequently he achieves independence by becoming known as a reliable and dependable musician to numerous contractors, a large group of composers and leaders, and the larger group of performing colleagues. As Becker states, a musician's reputation for dependability has economic value for those who request having that performer on their dates; and those who hire also have something at stake—a smooth, efficiently contracted group of free-lance musicians.[2] Making it means that one can be relied on. Despite the satisfaction of gaining some control over the conditions of hiring, many respondents were quick to point out that they are committed to take many calls they would prefer to turn down. Contractors will tolerate being turned down for only so long before they begin to look for other musicians. This is a contingency that is feared, or at least it gives rise to considerable apprehension, and perhaps an overemphasis on the value of being free from this constraint. Members of the inner circle are expected, for example, to take some bad work along with the good calls. If a contractor and leader provide a steady volume of calls, the performer is under obligation to remain loyal to them and take their work. Failing to do so would jeopardize his position in the inner circle, a valuable position that has been attained as a result of his reputation as a cool performer and his consistency in accepting any type of studio calls.

Finally, a cellist emphasized the concrete value of being in demand by a number of contractors, and his stronger bargaining position. Like several other respondents, he contrasted this considerable freedom with another stage in his career when he lacked the power to refuse, or to withdraw tactfully from, his principal contractor's calls.

Just two minutes before you came someone called me, a big contractor, and he said, "I have a call for you for June 12th,"

2. Becker, "Notes on the Concept of Commitment," *op. cit.*, p. 39.

and I said, "I don't think I can make it." He wanted to know why, so I told him I was going out of town for a week. He said, "You can't do that, the conductor wants you." Then he said, "I've got to have you." But I told him to get someone else. Now a few years ago I wouldn't have done that.

Q: And why is that?

Because to say you don't want to work, or you're tired or you want to take a vacation would have been a kiss of death. But now I don't care, I have enough work that if I antagonize a few people — so what? So now I'm more my own boss. Now I can bargain for money and conditions. In many cases, if someone wants me on a job and I'm busy on that day, they may change it to another day, or to the evening or so on. Everything is much more flexible.

Colleagues and Social Honor

Colleagues and contractors play an important role in respect to sponsorship. This is the major mechanism for controlling the timing and pacing of the recruit's climb up the studio escalator. The colleague-competitors are the performer's most supportive and critical audience. They use various benchmarks to judge each other. To construct those benchmarks they use several criteria which judge personal status and the worth of the work they are called on to perform. Unlike the situation in bureaucracies and more formally organized occupations, the rungs on the free-lance ladder are not neat bundles of power and privilege. The estimation of where one is cannot be made by a simple description of office or position. Rather, position is assessed in terms of a variety of evidence, such as the volume of calls from contractors, the type of work these calls entail, how much money the player makes, and what other colleagues say about him. The relative importance of significant others can be seen most easily if one looks at the members' language of invidious comparisons. In the interviews, place or social position is singled out linguistically; it is an important feature of the work mentality. "In" "outside," "a notch above," "just below," are common sense definitions of others' and one's own occupational rank. "The best musicians in town," "the busiest studio guys," "the concertmasters," "section men," "those out of the swim of things," are utterances of status distinctions. "Film work is the best" and "rock and roll dates are the worst" are clues to musicians' ideas of reputable and disreputable work. From the cognitive view of the musician, these are crucial ways of assessing his personal status.

As I have emphasized, social honor is typically expressed by a player's being recognized as an efficient player and tactful colleague. He can be counted on to handle the problematic contingencies arising at work. This recognition has its counterpart in the position he occupies on the contractors' lists, in the parts he plays in the orchestra, and in other advantages he may enjoy vis-a-vis others.

Making it implies, from this personal angle, that one has been victorious over other potential candidates, that one has made it at the expense of others also seeking to break into studio jobs. There are tendencies to social exclusiveness among those studio players most in demand. While a marked sense of pride in colleagues is evident in the interviews and conversations with free-lancers, those in "the inner circle" tended to emphasize and even exaggerate the talents of their colleagues. Three themes were threads in the linguistic fabric. First, emphasis was placed on the skills of those in high demand and, by implication, on one's own technical prowess. Second, playing calls with expert colleagues frequently blunted the impact of dull music, imcompetent conductors, degrading work situations, and unknowledgeable contractors. And third, these colleagues are seen as one's most valuable, critical, and supportive audience.

The first theme can be summed up with an observation heard time and time again: "I'm playing with the greatest group of musicians in this country." The second and third themes are interwoven in their phrase, "we play for each other." A few excerpts from the interviews illustrate the sentiment of camaraderie and personal honor.

Talking about both the status ranking of "inner circle" performers on his instrument and the time and effort required to continue making it in this group, a trumpet player told me about the personal side of his work contingencies.

> There are a number of top players in town on my instrument and I'd consider myself within the top 10 or 15, but it's a precarious list. You've got to keep up with those players and they are good, believe me they're fantastic. So you have to have good chops, you must be physically in shape, good ears, good vision, practice every day and put in a lot of energy outside the work. Anyone who thinks musicians just are working when they're in the studios is crazy, we're putting in two or three hours a day practicing. If I put as much time into architecture as I did into my horn, I'd be making over $80,000 a year. You have to compete with some great players; it's hard.

The performer is alert also to the approval of his working colleagues; unlike other performer-artists, they are artists without public audiences. They do not play for film viewers. With few exceptions, there was emphasis on pleasing fellow musicians rather than contractors, composers, or conductors.[3] The importance of colleagues and one's own standards were expressed in the phrase, "I play for myself and the guys in the orchestra." Within sections and from one orchestra section to another, colleague audiences are

---

3. For a similar picture see Warren Breed, "Social Control in the News Room: A Functional Analysis," *Social Forces* 33 (1955), pp. 326-335.

seen as most aware of performance problems, technical demands, subtleties in phrasing, command of the instrument, and poise under studio pressure. One string player described why fellow musicians were his best audience, and their applause the best reward on a studio date:

> I might work for weeks, but one day you turn the page and there is an excerpt from a very difficult concerto. I have to be ready to play it. As a matter of fact, your friend [a composer] once pulled something on me. He gave me a 16-bar introduction to a huge score – all by myself. I had to play it by sight. And of course I was delighted after the take because all the guys in the orchestra stood up and yelled *bravo* which is the *best* kind of applause you can get. What a feeling!

Performers who are soloists or top section men were likely to emphasize these more dramatic moments during recording takes. Others, though not hired for these positions, pointed out to me how pride in skills and the status conferred on their mastery were related. One saxophone-reed doubler, who within the past three years had become one of the most demanded players, described the prestige that is accorded to quality playing by reed section men:

> When the music is mediocre we play for one another. You try to do something outstanding for your colleagues, the guys in the section; you play for them and they acknowledge it if you play well – this is what makes it fun and always a source of amazement.

This allusion is to how, to put it informally, musicians amaze themselves: they "knock one another out" with fantastic dexterity, physical strength, and reading ability. Musicians in the same section, playing the same instruments, listen to one another daily under all types of recording conditions. Their knowledge about one another's skills is detailed, almost encyclopedic. Players in the same section can, if asked, endlessly spell out the strengths and weaknesses of colleagues. Some trumpet players are known for their finesse, their smooth legato style, and their soft attack; while others' reputations rest on bright tone, prowess in the upper register, and volume. Some cellists and violinists are cool and musically fault-less performers under the recording light, while others, though competent, have trouble coping with pressure. A number of reed doublers, while being able to play many reed instruments, were famous for their finesse on the flute, their oboe tone, or their jazz creativity on saxo-phone. These are differences of stylistic degree, not differences in competence. All have the basic skills re-quired to perform under recording conditions. But never-theless, some have different gifts (or are labelled as having such specializations by contractors) and are better at play-ing some kinds of music than others. Gaining a reputation among colleagues who play a similar instrument (one's most important peers) constitutes a most rewarding valu-able for a performer.

In stressing the role of colleagues' evaluations, the fol-lowing view indicates the way in which accorded social honor is a salient career valuable, at times more important than one's position on a contractor's list or reputation among composers or conductors.

> The esteem of your colleagues is what you work for and try to attain in the long run; they are the ones who know what you can do. I think respect from them will hold you in good stead much better than what the leaders or contractors think. To be recognized as one of the better musicians in town is very important.

Despite the self-serving nature of these remarks, es-teem is not enough. These mutual feelings of admiration for other performers' talents must be translated into con-crete acts, such as recommendations to contractors and leaders, if colleagues are to move into the higher-paying studio jobs. Because of the lopsided ratio of insiders to outsiders and the fact that potential members are all excellent musicians, selective hiring, like favoritism in sponsorship, can generate considerable animosity and strain between musicians, as well as between musicians and contractors.

All of these musicians are jealous of their talents; all have a considerable investment at stake. One result of the long years of training, internalized standards of excellence, and ego-involvement that go into the making of a musician is that competition for scarce rewards tends to sharpen the edges of social evaluation and to heighten the importance of signs of success. Machiavellian undertones are not far beneath the conversational surface when the musicians describe the disjunction they feel between their worth as performers (plus the considerable commitment to this self-image) and the position they enjoy in the free-lance hierarchy of calls. For example, I interviewed several musicians not in the inner circle, yet recognized by their colleagues as first-rate musicians; they resented their slow movement into the core of studio work. Few of them would support their colleagues' glowing remarks about the overriding value of social honor bestowed exclusively by other performers. Predictably, they grumbled about the lack of recommendations by other performers, despite the respect and esteem they felt they commanded. Clearly someone was to blame for their humiliation. They felt that their exclusion was due to the efforts to preserve the status and power of those already inside the studio circle. Because much of what goes on in hiring is accomplished through delicate negotiations and power plays, it is easy to see why many of these players whose careers are not as successful envision a monopoly of elite members calculating to sustain their own positions.

But behind the occupational facade of a community of

colleagues stands the considerable importance of sponsorship and the veto power of contractors and leaders. Regardless of a musician's talents, inclusion in the studio circle is not automatic, since long-term agreements between contractors and top players exist. Thus, the open nature of status conferral by colleagues conflicts with the closed, exclusive structure of the occupation. This accounts for the noted tendency of those outside to be less responsive when discussing the joys of colleague honor and to save some of their sharpest remarks for "rate busters," who "politic" to get work, those who "push their interests," "throw their weight around," or "bullshit" to be hired. The structure of the occupation encourages the perception of injustice by members who have staked their pride and self-esteem on making it in the studios, as well as on a career as a talented musician.

Dirty Work

Every line of work has its grubby jobs. Some occupations specialize in dirty work; others delegate socially disreputable activities to the lower-ranking members. The race track has its stable boys, the hospital its morgue attendants, social research its hired hands, apartments their janitors, and society its junk dealers, police, and executioners.[4] Free-lancers do not conceal their in-

4. Marvin Scott, *The Racing Game* (Chicago, Ill.: Aldine, 1968), Chapter 3; David Sudnow, *Passing On* (Englewood Cliffs, N. J.: Prentice-Hall, 1967); Julius Roth, "Hired Hand Research," *American Sociologist* 1 (August, 1966), 190–196; Raymond Gold, "In the Basement—The Apartment Building Janitor," chapter 1 in *The Human Shape of Work,* ed. by Peter Berger (New York: Free Press, 1964); Jack B. Ralph, "The Junk Business and the Junk Peddler" (unpublished M.A. thesis, University of Chicago, Department of Sociology, 1950); William A. Westley, "The Police: A Sociological Study of Law, Custom, and Morality" (unpublished Ph.D. dissertation, University of Chicago, Department of Sociology, 1951); Gerald D. Robin, "The Executioner: His Place in English Society," *British Journal of Sociology,* Vol. XV, September, 1964, 234–251.

dignation at having to play inept music under poor conditions. With obvious delight and sharp ridicule, one of the musicians we first interviewed left no doubt about what was "dirty" and what was "clean." At one point in the conversation, we were discussing some of his dissatisfactions with free-lancing. The language speaks for itself:

> Rock and roll, that's the lowest. The younger people produce the dates, so they experiment constantly, so they'll try this, then that, and then you sit there with the earphones on all day. You feel like a prostitute doing those types of dates. You come in there, and you're playing garbage, and you know the man's out to make money and he's selling crap to the teen market. That's probably the lowest form, the worst music. And then you have the obvious . . . well, for instance stupid TV shows where it's all obvious, funny little noises . . . it's not like a big, studio orchestra, on six sound tracks, where you can hear all the music on playback and it's great.

Judgments about good work contain explicit statements about those who compose and conduct it and the studios in which musicians play it. We find here the same criticisms of the handling of the score that are used to describe their problems at work. Here, however, the contingencies are placed in a moral order: "imaginative," "demanding," "the greatest," "challenging," and turning it around, "dull," "nothing," "the lowest," "just junk" are cues to music and musicians. Despite the variations in work, most found motion pictures their most interesting calls.[5] They particularly appreciated the time and care put into composition and recording. In the personal calculus of monotonous studio calls, films are much less repetitious and tedious.

---

5. Percentage distribution in responses to "Is the music any better in one area than in another?": Motion pictures, 43; television film, 1; both motion pictures and television film, 15; depends on composer, conductor, or studio, 25; no difference, 16.

The music is much better in pictures than any other type of thing. They take more time composing it, there's usually more money for it, they want a big-name composer to have the prestige attached to the film, and usually it demands more of your skill. It's not over and over again like TV film and like rock and roll you sit there and do the same tune over and many times can you play the same stuff, how many different ways are there? They can get away with the least possible, the cheapest music . . . they can disregard it. And let's see, rock and roll you sit there and do the same tune over and over, its maddening.

One type of repetitious hack work was especially annoying. The fad at several studios was to have bugle calls scattered throughout their TV westerns. For some of the brass players, this fashion was musically degrading, as one trumpet player indicated during the interview as he humorously ridiculed one of his steady, studio calls:

Television film is, at times, just dumb. Everybody apes the kind of music that is big at the moment. So one year it's western and by god every call it seems you play . . . [sings bugle call used in the old western cavalry charges] . . . and the next call . . . [sings it again]. . . . Then the next season it's detective type stuff, you know: hip, fast, and that's all you'll do. It's the same crap, the producer wants a show like B [popular TV show that ran several seasons with high ratings] but without B script, and B music, and the sponsor wants it so . . .

This is routine hack work. The style of the series creates it. Fashion has a lot to do with the music played. Each of these work settings has its disadvantages: rock and roll calls have endless takes and dull music; TV has insipid music and time pressures; and motion pictures add to these an elaborate technology.[6] As a collection of skills

6. Percentage distributions to "Are any studio calls dull and monotonous all of the time?": Motion pictures and television film, 11; Rock and roll recordings, 26; depends on the composer, 29; all or most of free-lance work, 13; all recordings, 9; "live TV, 4; none of it, 4; others, 4.

and activities, "dirty work" is important to study from the viewpoint of what studio players find happening to their skills. Some work is more favored than others; some is even more dignified, and increasing access to it is an important stage and turning point in the studio player's career. One reliable clue to position on the career ladder is simply the number of "good calls" a performer gets from hiring contractors. The number of motion picture and television film calls, commercial jingles, etc. is a measure of success and an occupational asset in itself. On these dates, also, the player is likely to find himself in the company of inner-circle or "cream of the crop" colleagues, another source of personal satisfaction. Escape from "dull" calls is therefore a tangible reward, a proof of good studio work. It is movement away from some jobs which are *infra dignitate*. It also implies career movement away from colleagues occupying lower positions on the rungs of the ladder. Climbing rungs on this moral division of studio labor is a form of investment which enhances the performer's commitment to commercial work.

With few exceptions, the respondents often reflected on a past career stage when they were obliged to take any type of contractors' calls in order to get started in the business. Moving into the better paying and more demanding studio dates accompanies an improvement of demand position in the lopsided hiring relationship.

> When I first started really working in town I felt I had to take everything; this is a big chance. Now I have more opportunity to choose and I don't have to put up with bad dates, record calls, rock and roll . . . anyway the music and money is better in television film and pictures.

Several of the studio composers and conductors noted similar sets of career signposts. One of their major advancement points comes when the composer demonstrates his ability to turn out scores under much time pressure. Once past this rite of passage, they report that the next step involves moving from television scores to full-length motion picture films, especially those with larger budgets and more opportunity to write. For both performer and composer, one problem was the fear that they may become "frozen" at a particular level of work, or fall behind in the race to move just as rapidly as other colleagues into better work.

To those musicians outside the studio work, these problems could appear to be an embarrassment of musical and financial riches. In comparison to playing weddings, dances, nightclub casuals, pick-up band jobs, and other non-studio routine work, such status and colleague struggles might seem trivial. However, one only has to remember that each individual uses the norms and taken-for-granted world of his colleague group as a signpost or yardstick against which to measure his own progress, and by which to solve his own work problems. As Hughes and his students have reminded us, any line of work has its "bad gigs" and dumb jobs. The concepts of work problems, colleague competition, control over autonomy at work, and socially disreputable work can be usefully employed not only in studying the music business, and other occupations within the mass-media industries, but the drama of work in general.

CHAPTER SEVEN

The Studio Pro's Perspectives

Free-lance performers face various situational contingencies in their everyday calls. Some are routine and expected; others are capricious and unanticipated. As they interact with contractors, composers, leaders, and their colleagues, the musicians acquire valuables which are difficult to abandon. Making it implies gaining access to the rewards the studios have to offer. Growing demand by contractors and others is tangible proof of good work and successful playing. Skillful negotiation of the rungs on the career ladder indicates comparative success over others. And the more he is in demand, the more influence and credit the musician has in the bargaining strategies with those who hire him.

A common frame of reference develops around these patterns of collective activity. The coordinated sets of ideas and actions that these performers use in successfully handling the problematic features of their work in the free-lance setting is called their perspective.[1] Studio work

1. Howard S. Becker, Blanche Geer, Everett C. Hughes, and Anselm L. Strauss, *Boys in White: Student Culture in Medical School* (Chicago: University of Chicago Press, 1961), pp. 34-36; Howard S.

is defined as a business. Money is this occupation's most compelling asset; the pursuit of cash forms the rationale behind the free-lancer's actions and, correspondingly, this business perspective is sustained by success. Ideas and actions mutually reinforce one another. This perspective arises not only from situational features of the occupation itself, but also from the understandings people bring with them to this setting. A distinction can be made between long-range and immediate perspectives. The business perspective, their attempts at and ideas about maximizing income, is linked to beliefs formed prior to getting into the studios; it is a result of their definitions of going commercial and the shared meanings this experience has for them. But at the same time, once in this setting, the performer finds himself facing specific problems generated by the socio-technical system of free-lance work. In response to these features, the meaning of money is shaped by interaction with other objects in his experience, such as what is happening to his skills and his career, and the personal status he has gained in the informal organization of work. This situational, short-run, business perspective emerges as a collective solution to immediate contingencies.[2]

The pro's perspective cannot be understood simply as a response to the studio scene. Nor can it be viewed as a direct reflection of the attitudes musicians bring with them from orchestras, big bands, jazz and concert circuits, and other career lines. This chapter focuses on how the business perspective is tied to past experiences, immediate constraints, and the fear of future deprivation. An elective affinity links these ideas and actions. The emphasis on

Becker, Blanche Geer, and Everett C. Hughes, *Making the Grade: The Academic Side of College Life* (New York: John Wiley & Sons, Inc., 1968).

2. Long-range and short-range perspectives are used in Howard S. Becker, Blanche Geer, Everett C. Hughes, and Anselm L. Strauss, *Boys in White, op. cit.,* pp. 35–36, 68–79, 431.

making money, as noted, is a response to the problematic features of free-lance work whose meaning cannot be understood outside of the total round of the musician's taken-for-granted world. We have noted that the nature of this perspective is influenced by the performer's prior orientations and understandings brought into this setting. Thus, some of these musicians attempt to build their demand in free-lance work and make enough money to be in a position to turn down degrading jobs, or those calls which would not affirm their identity as musicians. The meaning of money, in this case, must be seen as an instance of piling up occupational insurance in order to maintain some control over what work to do, the disposition of leisure and work time.[3] Such ideas are formed outside the studios and make up the diffuse and generalized understandings musicians bring with them.

Money is the major institutionalized valuable in the studios. Each musician defines the making of income as a most important component of his work experience and the major source of satisfaction in being a free-lance performer.[4] This immediate business perspective describes

3. See Everett C. Hughes, *Men and Their Work* (Glencoe, Ill.: Free Press, 1958) p. 55.
4. Percentage responses to what free-lancers like best about being free-lance musicians:

| | Response Sequence | | | |
	First	Second	Third	Total
Money	31	19	29	26
The Freedom*	29	15	7	21
Variety of Work†	23	17	–	18
Colleagues	5	21	43	15
Musical Challenge	7	11	7	10
Leisure	–	17	14	8
Nothing	5	–	–	2
	100	100	100	100
	(65)	(53)	(14)	(134)

* "I'm my own boss," "Freedom to choose my work," etc.
† Variety of music, composers, conductors, situations, etc.

the work and career situation in which free-lancers find themselves, the rewards they expect from their work, the actions appropriate to the meeting of this end, and a relevant set of criteria by which colleagues are judged.

While these respondents use a wide-angle lens in describing their work experiences in terms of personal dignity as a musician, status among their colleagues, control over conditions of work, etc., the maximization of income is the primary focal point in their collective perspective. It shapes the contour of commitment to work as well as being a convenient way of expressing just how well the performer has handled the problematic features of the studios. It is not unlike the enemy insignia on the side of a fighter pilot's cockpit, or the notches on the handle of a gunman's weapon; the volume of studio calls and entries onto the bank ledger tally a record of achievement, a measurement of success over colleague competitors. Cash also smooths the disagreeable aspects of many studio calls. The integration of these various components of work around the business perspective is seen in the following excerpt from an interview with a successful pro. His language is representative of every studio player interviewed, particularly in response to the difficult question about the meaning they attach to their employment. At this point in the interview, he was talking about some of the dull calls he was obliged to accept every week.

There are times when you can be rather bored with your work. Maybe it's the fact that I'm doing what I want to do and making a lot of money at it that I can sit there and be bored. But it's not dull all of the time. When it is, there's always that little carrot and it's that I earn, on the average, 30, 35 bucks an hour, and so it's the financial aspect of it that has the most meaning to me.

Q: I see, that's the meaning. Anything else?

I consider myself very fortunate that I'm as successful as I am in it. To me it's strictly a business, that's its meaning. And as I said before, at times I enjoy it, when I get to play a solo, working with a fine composer, an efficient conductor. At times it's rather dull, but you're also under a lot of pressure and when it happens the challenge is there. . . . I think it's enabling me to lead the kind of life that I want and also I can pick and choose a little more as the years go by. I'm finding myself in a position where if I decide that I'm working too much, I just take off. I'm very happy with the work I'm doing; very happy.

Work contingencies induce extreme sensitivity to the competitive position of each entrepreneur. Money is a shorthand for the performer's social worth in the hiring market. Given the fluctuations in studio productions, fads and fashions in styles, and other contingencies set in motion by this rather unpredictable industry, musicians experience a diffuse tension about their present and future economic rewards. Not uncommonly, each player was prone to quickly translate references of skill and status to their pecuniary implications.

I'd say the best thing about free-lance is the different types of music; we play everything, some of it is great. Also aside from the money, I'm one of those who has enough technique to be one of the first ten players on my instrument in town. So, essentially I'm doing the top work now, both musically and, of course, income-wise. It's the most lucrative work. There's no place to go from Hollywood.

To the extent that studio free-lancers perceive their work and careers as problematic, their reaction is influenced by their ideas of what is causing these problems. The predominant point of view focuses on market pressures acting on the studios, and these pressures are then filtered through the social apparatus of contractors, composers, leaders, and colleagues. As one brass player put it, "This is one big crap shoot; we never know what will happen from year to year." Making comparatively big money is a convenient indicator of one's personal worth on the studio stock exchange. It is also a convenient symbol of one's control over some of the conditions of powerlessness a musician finds himself in vis a vis contractors, studio budgets, and on individual studio calls.

In the light of his concerns with gaining some control over the conditions of hiring, the musician's economic and business outlook takes on a more complex shape. An underlying and persistent theme which runs throughout these chapters is the correspondence between money and enlargement of discretion. In his *Philosophie des Geldes,* Simmel devotes part of his analysis to an explanation of the conditions under which money increases freedom. First, it liberates the social actor from excessive obligations to others, and second, it expands the opportunities for him to express his will.[5] The business perspective and the meaning which free-lance musicians attach to remunerative rewards is not solely anchored in cash itself. As an object of social value, and as a scarce commodity, its meaning derives from, in Simmel's words, the "reciprocal relation which is set up among several objects by virtue of these qualities, each defining the other, and each giving back to the other the meaning which it receives from it."[6] Specifically, the currency of such evaluation is the economic success a studio player enjoys and the corresponding success in having power to avoid the more distasteful constraints of work. Several lines of evidence, many of which have already been presented, point to the importance of these reciprocal relations.

5. Georg Simmel, *Philosophie des Geldes,* 2nd ed. (Leipzig: Duncker und Humblot, 1907); "Money and Freedom," in Robert H. Park and Ernest W. Burgess, *Introduction to the Science of Sociology* (Chicago: University of Chicago Press, 1921), pp. 552–53; see also Donald N. Levine, "The Structure of Simmel's Social Thought," in *Essays on Sociology, Philosophy and Aesthetics,* edited by Kurt H. Wolff (New York: Harper and Row, Torchbook, 1965), pp. 9–32.
6. Simmel, *Philosophie des Geldes, op. cit.,* p. 61.

First, while the pursuit of money is an all-important goal for these respondents, many gave elaborate reasons why they, in fact, turn down some high-paying jobs. One obvious reason was pointed out in the preceding chapters: free-lancers take pride in being free. This typically means free from contractors' absolute power. Keeping several irons in the fire and spreading accounts among contractors give the performer a series of discretionary strategies for spreading risk as well as maximizing choices.

Second, high-paying studio calls are turned down at times just because of inept composers and conductors. Again, a turning point in one's career comes when the player has made it to a position where he can afford to do this. An inner circle bass player put it this way:

> I like the freedom. I make enough money now, if I wish to turn them down, I'm not obligated to anyone. Now we can pick our calls a little more, not so much of those rock and roll dates that can go on all day. I don't like those so I try to avoid them because I'm secure enough with a number of contractors so I don't have to take every call and end up playing for some of these guys.

And third, inner circle team members often turn down high-paying work because of other players on the date. While collectively all are in the same boat, some are preferred more than others as performing colleagues. Performing with desired colleagues and significant others is a major reward often sought by those who have the luxury of choice.

In short, knowing that these respondents give priority to high-level remunerative returns does not complete the picture they have of their work. Once a performer has made it, and is getting a desired level of economic reward, he does not necessarily seek less from his work experience. I disagree with Dubin and others who point out that to the extent men choose to define their work as largely a means to extrinsic ends, they are not likely to look for or expect much else from what they do for a living.[7] The pro's perspective is, indeed, a calculative one: studio work is a means to ends outside the setting. But it is also more than this. The musician who sees his work primarily as a means to extrinsic ends is not likely to look to his colleagues as a source of social support and pride; nor is he likely to express considerable resentment over the degrading music he is called upon to play, or search out and try to maximize those studio conditions which affirm his identity as a musician. On the contrary, it appears that once the player has made it up the precarious rungs of the studio ladder and once his economic expectations are met, he finds a measure of comparative success in being able to choose his calls and maximize, within the constraints of free-lance bargaining procedures, other more intrinsic ends. The reciprocal relations between money, comparative freedom, and opportunity to sustain personal standards of superior performance indicate that, while they are committed to their employment in terms of economic returns, free-lance work is nevertheless more than "strictly a business." This short-run situational perspective is, in turn, shaped by the understandings performers bring with them to the studios.

Much of the substantive material dealing with long-range perspectives has been discussed. We shall now look briefly at the interplay between long-range and immediate perspectives, particularly the impact of prior ideas in shaping the musicians' businesslike response to free-lance work.

Goldthorpe and his associates have pointed to the important role of expectations and understandings workers

7. Robert Dubin, "Industrial Workers' Worlds: A Study of the 'Central Life Interests' of Industrial Workers," *Social Problems* 3, 1956, 131–142.

bring with them into an occupation; they argue that often too great a weight is placed on technological factors as determinants of work attitudes.[8] Particularly in studies of assembly-line workers, members' concern for income and maximization of economic advantage are taken as indicators of work "alienation." C. Wright Mills, in discussing union ideology, makes the same argument when he holds that the slogan of, in his words, "alienated work (is) more and more money for less and less work."[9] He goes on to say that income has become the major goal of workers and white-collar employees because of the loss of craftsmanship, autonomy, and meaningful control over work. Similarly, Blauner points out that instrumental work attitudes, a concern for security and pay, are a major indicator of self-estrangement and alienation.[10] In other words, these studies locate the predominantly instrumental orientation to work in members' responses to the situation. Perspective is seen as *consequence* of work structure.

In contrast, the experiences of studio musicians suggests that the priority given to economic rewards was part of a long-range perspective in fact *causative* of their present situation and the meaning free-lancers gave to their studio employment. Here is a young reed player who

8. John H. Goldthorpe, David Lockwood, Frank Bechhofer, and Jennifer Platt, *The Affluent Worker: Industrial Attitudes and Behavior* (London: Cambridge University Press, 1968); in this and the following paragraphs I am indebted to John H. Goldthorpe's discussion in "Attitudes and Behavior of Car Assembly Workers," *British Journal of Sociology* XVII (September, 1966), 227-244. The impact of prior orientations on present definitions of situation has important theoretical implications as I have pointed out, see Chapters 1 and 3.

9. C. Wright Mills, *White Collar* (New York: Oxford University Press, Galaxy Books, 1956) p. 230.

10. Robert Blauner, *Alienation and Freedom: The Factory Worker and His Industry* (Chicago: University of Chicago Press, 1964), p. 119.

moved into the studio in his mid-twenties and is now making over sixty thousand dollars a year.

In my twenties, I decided that from the standpoint of a business, the only attractive business of the musician [sic] would be a studio musician. If I took a backward look I would find that there was no possible way for me to earn the money that I could in any other field. It was a necessity, in other words, I couldn't think of anything else that I could do at this point, this was my career. So I decided to try to get into the best end of the business.

Q: What part did your family, your getting married, play in this?

It shaped my thinking; it changed my thinking of music into a business rather than into a thing I just do for fun. because of the responsibilities involved for the family. That made a big difference. If I went out to do and play just what I wanted to do and play, I wouldn't necessarily be a studio musician, I don't think. But if I wanted to earn as much money as I could, there's no question, that's the only field where you can earn this kind of money. I would like to continue and possibly semi-retire at a rather early age. But I'd like to have other interests, I'd like to do some playing. Being a free-lance musician means that you're available to work at all hours, anywhere, at any time, and you have to be your own judge as to when to stop. How do you do it gracefully? There is a way, we just tell them we're busy, that's all.

Like his colleague above, the next musician, an inner-circle string player, pointed out that the decision to make money was made at the expense of several intrinsic, but low-paying, types of musical jobs. For him, the implication of being forced into studio work was particularly degrading. What is important here is that his "devaluation" of commercial work is a generalized dissatisfaction and anger at society for not supporting music; he is clearly mad at the entire business of music.

Let's face it, I came out here because I would have to work twice as hard for half as much money. So I just shut my mind to all of that. I had compensating factors, not artistically, but money-wise. I know it's a hell of a way to look at it, but these are the facts of life. It's a way of making a buck, one of the *only* ways in this society for the musician. My only satisfaction is from my earnings. Christ, if I were only making twelve or fifteen thousand a year, I'd probably go nuts.

Q: Did commercial music and playing in the setting disillusion you in any way?

No, I knew what it was.

Q: What?

Well, I think of what comes to mind and I think of my colleagues and their eyes would pop if they heard the word, but it's sort of a prostitution. I'm saying it objectively. I think commercial music is a selling of a birthright, really. All my colleagues have such a gift that it's a'shame that we all have to become cynical in terms of returns for an artistic endeavor. In other words, I think the vast concentration of fine musicians out here is testimonial to the fact that they see music not as they would like it, but as it is.

This generalized mood directs dissatisfaction at the problematic features of earning a living in music rather than the specific "alienating" components of the studios. The source of their markedly instrumental or businesslike perspective is linked to their career problems, position in the life cycle, family responsibilities, and the like. In other words, this study does not support the frequent characterization of "alienated labor" or the theme of "selling out" offered by students of mass society insofar as it links attitudes to work structure exclusively. Our starting point has been the long-range perspective and careers of these musicians, rather than the technological system of the studios. The musicians' definitions of the studio situation are in large part shaped by understandings and subjective meanings formed prior to present situational employment.

Generalized long-range perspectives brought to the commercial scene mediate between the structural features of work and the performers' attitudes towards what happens to their skills, the status they enjoy among their colleagues, and the evaluations of their worth. An important component which shapes their beliefs and behavior is the pride these performers have in themselves and their talents *in general*. They do not lose this long-range perspective but develop a blasc, even cynical, stance towards their everyday calls. While good music, music that affirms the use of their skills, is anticipated, it is not greatly missed if absent. It is a sort of bonus. They simultaneously maintain an identity of themselves as musicians, which has its origin in their training and careers, and a situational view of themselves as free-lancers which sees only the immediate problems generated by studio calls. One finds, for example, the broader criterion for judging and evaluating work performance expressed in terms of whether the work affirms their own standards of superior playing. Phrases such as "I play for myself" and "we play for our colleagues" sum up this wider understanding which they see as relevant, and possible to use in the studios. This concern for and self-attachment to quality performance overrides the contingencies and fluctuating demands of free-lance work. Thus, their attitudes are not an automatic response to the deprivations of recording technology and the division of labor. In coming to terms with this immediate situation, both economic and musical ideas are used and influence short-range perspectives.

The requirements and pressures of their immediate situation nevertheless have an important impact on free-lancers. It is the business of making money and getting on with a career that alarms critics of the commercial scene. These respondents are hard-nosed realists; they fear potential erosion of the valuables they have accumulated during their career climb to the top of the occupational ladder. Practical considerations such as the power of contractors and composers and the potential danger of losing their accounts exert a sobering influence on the use of manipulative strategies designed to control the personal side of free-lance bargaining. Knowing that contractors can always turn cool and choose other solid players increases the reluctance to be overly choosy and heightens the willingness, albeit grudging, to take what they get. The luxury of making it is having some choice at one's command.

Other considerable risks are generated by the market itself and bring about institutional pressures in the short-range situation. A jettisoned television series reminds these musicians less of the degrading music they had to play on the call than of their extreme vulnerability to the decisions of producers. A production which starts cutting back on the music budget reminds them of their susceptibility to slipping Nielsen ratings and belt tightenings at the studio.

Their long-range perspective, and the view they have of themselves as musicians, is accommodated to the pressure-filled problems of making a good living in the business and protecting themselves against the hazards of bad times in the future. The collective attempts to build occupational insurance against competitors, threatening market fluctuations, and the studios' economic performance are responses to the present situation as well as to the unpredictable future. In this way, business perspectives formed in adaptation to the immediate studio scene mesh with past experiences and develop into actions and beliefs about future problems.

CHAPTER EIGHT

Concluding Observations

The aims of this study have been to describe and to analyze the occupational perspectives and career lines of commercial free-lance musicians. This concluding section examines the findings in a broader context. It returns to the themes which began the study: work problems and the structure of occupational perspectives, and a related critique of mass society, in particular a critique of artists who work in popular-culture occupations and industries.

We began by asking if the presumed sociological relationship between the artist and society, as portrayed in the mass-culture literature, is factually correct. Two related features come to the forefront of these writings about man and mass-media occupations. Both are closely tied to a critique of modern work. They are (1) an unfavorable assessment of the personal consequences of commercial work borrowed from the image of assembly-line production, and (2) the implicit model of man as individual creator and artist. While these features are not found in all discussion of mass culture, they nevertheless represent a set of perspectives that delineate what these critics see as happening to certain performing and creative artists.

Commercial Work and the Assembly Line

The occupational setting with the most degrading consequences appears to be a favorite model for the critique
of the mass-media, mass-entertainment industries. This is
part of a broader argument which notes the alienating
effects of routinized work on the individual, and in particular on the creative artist whose skills and judgments
are employed in the service of "non-artistic" aims. Herbert Gans sums up this perspective:

> The criticism of the process of popular-culture creation
> breaks down into three charges: that mass culture is an in-
> dustry organized for profit; that in order for this industry to
> be profitable, it must create a homogeneous and standardized
> product that appeals to a mass audience; and that this re-
> quires a process in which the industry transforms the creator
> into a worker on a mass production assembly line, where he
> gives up the individual expression of his own skills and
> values.[1]

Throughout this work we were interested in the contingencies of free-lance employment for these musicians, and
in the fascinating problem of highly skilled and talented
performers working in a setting which resembled an assembly line, or at least a highly organized industry having
some of these features. As we proceeded, it became
apparent that this view was overdrawn. While film production is a highly organized and technical process which
shares features of assembly-line work — predetermined
pacing in accord with the film action, minute subdivision
of the product, and in many instances a repetitiveness of
the film — the charge that the "dream factory's" productions are consistently perceived as standardized and dominated by a technology which downgrades skills is an exag-
geration. From the perspective of the musicians in-

1. "Popular Culture in America: Social Problems in a Mass Society
or Social Asset in a Pluralistic Society?" in *Social Problems: A Modern
Approach,* Ed. by H. Becker (New York: Wiley, 1966).

terviewed, many of the problematic features of their studio work stem from the inherent variety and unpredictability of the scores that they play for the sound tracks. The alienating consequences are neither consistent nor uniform in their effects. Again, the term "contingency" best sums up studio work and free-lance employment in general. The changing features of the musicians' work reflect the varying demands placed on them as different composers and conductors with varying skills and talents determine what the musician will play. As they put it, "You never know what they'll throw at you." Work demands are variable, being contingent upon budget allotment for music, time given for scoring and performance, the level of predetermined pacing, and the difficulty of an individual musical part. This is not a description of the work role of an assembly-line worker, as found in Walker and Guest's classic monograph.[2]

We can look at music in the film industry as a spectrum running from extremely dull and routine to exciting and challenging. At one end of this spectrum the musician relinquishes the individual expression and unfolding of his own skills since the music is degrading, the film uninteresting, and the conductor incompetent. At the other end of the spectrum we find instances where a composer has been given the time to write a challenging score, a piece of music which places musical and technical demands on the performers. Paradoxically, studio work demands that the player always be at the top of his technical ability while frequently downgrading the use of his talents. It is precisely this first band of the spectrum which many assume to be an accurate description of the film production is the " . . . denigration of the talented by the untalented,"[3] or in

    2. Charles R. Walker and Robert H. Guest, *The Man on the Assembly Line* (Cambridge: Harvard University Press, 1952).
    3. Hortense Powdermaker, *Stranger and Friend: The Way of an Anthropologist* (New York: W. W. Norton, 1966), p. 226.

Dwight Macdonald's statement that "mass culture is imposed from above. It is fabricated by technicians hired by businessmen."[4] Implicit in these charges is a comparison of popular culture with the creation of "high culture" which, in Gans' words, ". . . is portrayed as noncommercial . . . non-standardized . . . and encouraging a creative process whereby an individual creator works to achieve his personal ends more than those of an audience."[5] This final point is an interesting and important one. Let us examine it in more detail, for it is an outlook generally shared by several theorists.

Man as Artist, Worker as Creator

The image of man as creator, as an artificer, inventor, and craftsman who shapes his work from idea to execution is foremost not only in the critique of popular culture but is also a foundation of Mills' indictment of modern work—the loss of the craftsmanship ideal—as it was a basis of Karl Marx's analysis of alienated labor. In this view, man fights to preserve his autonomy in the face of modern industrial society, which radically lowers his skills through mechanization, standardization, and the division of labor. We have attempted to determine under what conditions the tendencies outlined by Marx, Mills, and the "mass culture" theorists are intensified for a group of musicians who are one part of an elaborately organized set of industries. It is appropriate at this point to briefly explore some assumptions underlying this image of man and the perspectives of these players. The conception of the artist-creator by which intellectuals evaluate certain kinds of work is somewhat removed from the views of our respondents. It would be a descriptive error to sum up

4. Dwight Macdonald, "A Theory of Mass Culture," in Bernard Rosenberg and David M. White, eds., *Mass Culture: The Popular Arts in America* (New York: Free Press, 1957), pp. 59–73, quote on p. 60.
5. Gans, "Popular Culture," *op. cit.* p. 554.

their views by simply stating that they are "frustrated artists," alienated in their work because they are not autonomous creators. The content of their dissatisfactions is largely concrete and pragmatic rather than ideal; it is even prosaic: contractors with too much power, bad composers, studio pressures, political infighting, etc. Having shown that besides these feelings of discontent there are balancing elements of intense pride in their skill and confidence in their abilities *in general,* we would conclude that these players have "adapted." We could even say that they have "split the difference" between their material interests and artistic ideals. These ideals, however, are radically different from those of the creator-as-artist. This model is more appropriate for jazz musicians, blues singers, composers, poets, writers, painters, and some intellectuals.

This ideal of work is misleading because it assumes interests and occupational problems typically encountered by a select group of artists in our society, namely, those engaged in creative rather than interpretive functions.[6] To those not familiar with studio work, the musicians' job may look routine; they are "technicians" when contrasted with a model of the artist as "individual creator." Without engaging in elaborate abstract formulations, a distinction can be made between the individual and the collective role. These two terms have their counterparts: the creative and interpretive role. The tendency to identify any commercial work—taking place in a division of labor and being non-autonomous—as alienating is at the heart of the mass-culture critique. It helps to account for the critics' belief that such employment is undesirable to the artist. Following this line of argument, we would expect the conflict between the "artist" and the "mass-culture in-

6. Talcott Parsons, *The Social System* (New York: Free Press, 1964), p. 408.

dustry" to be minimized among performers, for example, such as musicians in comparison with other, more traditionally individualistic creative roles, such as writer-poets, composers, painters, sculptors, even photographers.

This distinction indicates that many types of occupations cannot be conveniently fitted into the "alienated artist" framework without flattening the contours of occupational problems and their impact on inner experience.

On a more general level, the point which has been emphasized throughout is that the perspective a member has on his occupation derives from a complex interaction between his material and ideal interests. One investigator has concluded that the trend is towards more discontent with work, or at least apathy towards the work experience. Pride in creative work is now shared by an increasing number of poeple due to increased education which instills members of society with the belief that their work "should be" creative and self-fulfilling.[7] But at the same time the realities of the work environments preclude, in many ways, the realization of these ideals.[8] Some have argued that leisure will become increasingly important as a primary life interest. Although we have not developed this theme, we should point out that almost all of the musicians interviewed here find creative outlets outside their studio work: in community orchestras, recitals, jazz dates, as well as the more "high-brow" recordings often made on the West Coast.[9] In fact, at the time of

7. Blauner, "Work Satisfaction and Industrial Trends in Modern Society," R. Bendix and S. M. Lipset, Eds., *Class, Status and Power* (New York: Free Press of Glencoe, 1966), p. 486.

8. A similar theme is found in Griff's "Commercial Artist," in Stein, *et al., Identity and Anxiety: Survival of the Person in Mass Society* (Glencoe, Ill: Free Press, 1960), pp. 219–241.

9. About three-quarters of our entire sample were active in chamber symphonies, quartets, or occasional jazz gigs outside of their free-lance studio work. Some of these players taught at the colleges and universities in the Los Angeles area.

this writing several of these musicians had gone on the road with famous jazz groups, returned from a summer of engagements in Europe as soloists, or participated in other types of "leisure" which they felt they "had to do." It bears mentioning that some of our findings are of essentially historical interest. The subjective dispositions described in these pages were shaped by relatively unique historical events; the musicians' experiences in, and perceptions of, their careers are, in a sense, social histories which bear the imprint of the Depression and war years. They are musicians of their particular generation(s), whose careers unfolded during times when commercial employment was economically attractive in theater orchestras (late 1920's), during the expansion of radio as well as large night-club orchestras (1930's and 1940's), and later during the studio orchestras in Hollywood (1940's). The war altered many potential symphony careers since fewer positions were available after the war when the player returned to civilian life; the big bands of the forties went into historical decline following the war, and with them their unique opportunities.

The research has been deliberately focused on those with preferred positions in the informal structure of free-lance work, those who make themselves available and actively pursue studio work and who, in turn, are sought after by those who hire and recommend. They are more likely to be the "old pros," whose status derives from their past performances—their reliability and efficiency—and structural position in a relatively closed, even monopolistic, work organization. This raises some questions of substantive import. Namely, are the findings specific only to this sector of older "inner circle" musicians? What of those without such backgrounds? While we have no definite answers to these questions, several trends can be mentioned with certainty.

First, a small number of these musicians are under 38 (9 out of 73); they were in their twenties and beginning to establish their careers during the 1950's. Historically they are set apart from their older colleagues, although the data do not permit generalizations about differences in kind between them. In degree the younger players differ slightly from the older ones: (1) younger players tend to be more satisfied with commercial work, in the main because they have recently made it — or have begun to make significant footholds — in a highly competitive setting; (2) they appear to report that they aimed to be studio musicians earlier than the older musicians did. This obviously reflects the historical fact that there are comparatively fewer big bands for the brass, saxophone, percussion, and even bass players than in the 1940 era. And the responses of potential symphony players suggest less commitment to an orchestra career than their older colleagues probably had at a similar age. It is my impression that for these younger players, the older prescribed career line of college-conservatory training followed by entry into a minor orchestra is no longer automatic. These, then, constitute differences in degree. Considerations of actual opportunities, economics, and even the attraction of the studios in terms of colleagues are seen as having influences on the timing of career plans as well as on the course of action.

Second, 14 of our respondents are not in the "inner circle" of motion picture and television film work. Their calls are split between film work, record dates, live and taped television programs and transcriptions (jingles), as well as various casual calls. While they do some film work, the largest part of their yearly income comes from a combination of free-lance activities (less than 40 per cent of their income is from film studio calls). Again they differ only in degree. Those who work most of the rock and roll dates in Los Angeles persistently complain about the mo-

notony of these calls; they have what could be called the
ad nauseum syndrome: "takes" done over and over again.
They contrasted the variety and skill demands of film
work with doing "Top 40" tunes. In their dissatisfaction
with dull music, powerful contractors, bad composers, and
orchestrators, their language and style was identical with
that of those in the film area. The majority wished that
they could do more film work; discontent with the current
rock scene and with the sitting around and waiting during
"live taping" of TV shows were continually and spontan-
eously mentioned by these musicians. The reader should
be advised, then, that proportionally more of these musicians are dissatisfied than those in the "inner circle,"
which points to some of the important differences in work
attitudes by type of work and position in free-lance im-
ployment.

Third, 19 per cent (14) of those interviewed entered
commercial work in Los Angeles during the period after
the contract orchestras, after 1958. Some of them are in
the "inner circle" and others are not. Our discussion of
career contingencies based on breaking into free-lance
studio setting nevertheless holds for the majority of
this sample. Sponsorship is crucial, or was crucial both in
the contract days as well as in the present, and many of
the same career contingencies still exist. We can, however, only speculate about the influence of studio-contract
experiences, such as yearly security, present work perspectives, and the exigencies of free-lance hiring with its
lack of security. Many were clearly dissatisfied with
present hiring arrangements and their lack of control over
their working conditions; fewer still, however, wished a
return to contracts and when asked why, they indicated
that money had almost unqualified priority. They complain about it, but few within the "inner circle" desired the
cut in yearly pay which a return to studio security would
involve.

Despite some differences we find variations about a single outlook for these musicians. Rather than a large diversity of perspectives, the differences are essentially of degree rather than of kind. While the intrinsic nature of their jobs is important to them, as expressed by their delight in playing musically interesting calls, the intense pride in skills, and the importance of colleagues' opinions about their professional abilities, the meaning of work derives from an essentially monetary set of attitudes. These interests were shaped by the person's career aspirations and actual work experiences prior to this type of employment and, once in it, were reinforced by the structure of the occupation.

Sorting through the transcribed interviews for a final time produced persistent reminders of the larger context in which our musicians' careers have taken place. With the data available to us, we believe the areas explored in these pages to be of significance on a more general level. One way to summarize is to suggest that the mass-society, mass-culture theory and Marxian theory overestimate the degree of work alienation because of their view of work itself—the craftsman-artist model of work—and the consequences of labor—consistent dehumanization of the person's involvement from the impact of the production process. The study suggests an alternative image of our mass-culture industries and their occupations, one that does not underestimate the varieties of the working experience and the subtleties of situational adjustment by which, in this case, musicians come to terms with their world of work. While the problems of the performing artist in this country and the pull of commercial work are too broad for us to broach at this point, it should be appreciated that these respondents were not forced into studio work because of a lack of talent or skill which would have kept them from moving into more "musically intrinsic" types of employment. At least one important implication of our findings is that these recording musicians' lack of commitment to "high culture" (to use a phrase of the critics) or their work "alienation" (judged by the priority given to income) must be sought not only in the social and technological organization of work, but also in the wider society. Despite the emphasis given to occupational structure in the neo-Marxian writings, the present data raise doubts about the exclusive priority of this argument in describing work perspectives and the social-psychological career adjustments made by people in our society.

Placed alongside our data, a recent Twentieth Century Fund study by William J. Baumol and William G. Bowen reports that consumers in this country pay around 11 cents out of every $100 of disposable income on the performing arts, that the median income of male musicians and music teachers in 1959 was a little under $4,800,[10] and that as late as the 1964–65 season, the average salary of musicians in the 25 major orchestras was $5,267 for a season of about 30 weeks.[11] The fact that this figure represents a 20 per cent rise from the earnings two years earlier underscores some of the financial problems high-culture settings, and their artists, are facing today.

The personal side of this economic problem may be summed up best by quoting two musicians, a string player 50 years old, who was clearly one of the more dissatisfied musicians in our sample, and then a brief statement by the master, Igor Stravinsky.

After a long harangue about his unhappy experiences in one symphony, our studio player paused and seemed to have lost his train of thought, then he began again with considerable emotion:

10. Baumol and Bowen, *Performing Arts: The Economic Dilemma* (New York: Twentieth Century Fund, 1966), p. 301.

11. *Ibid*, p. 107.

... and I don't know what started this, but again it's one of those things where I feel that a live musician is simply not appreciated enough. In the art of music ... society has no idea of the suffering, the harassment, the stupidity. I would say the culture of this country is being supported by the musicians, not the wealthy, but the musicians. We have subsidized it, and I resent it no end, so that, I said, the only answer I've found is in the commercial end of things. I have a background of contempt for the way symphony musicians are treated. At least I can play what I want, and have some financial stability.

Let me say, once and for all, that I have never regarded poverty as attractive; that I do not wish to be buried in the rain, unattended, as Mozart was; that the very image of Bartok's poverty-stricken demise, to mention only one of my less fortunate colleagues, was enough to fire my ambition to earn every penny that my art would enable me to extract from the *society* that failed in its duty toward Bartok as it had earlier failed with Mozart.

(from *Themes and Episodes*)[12]

These arguments might serve to edify the critics of popular culture and those who see any economic motive in the service of the performing arts as a degradation, as a sell-out, and as a loss of internal purity.

12. Igor Stravinsky, with Robert Craft, *Themes and Episodes* (Alfred A. Knopf, 1966), p. 91.

Methodological Appendix A: Sample and Methods

The following sections set forth some of the techniques, strategies, and logic of operations through which the data were gathered. Appendix A presents the final methods and techniques employed, the sample, and its special characteristics. A more personal history of the research is found in Appendix B that shows some of the stages and problems encountered in moving the investigation from a rather "loose" set of interests and hunches to mustering evidence for ideas about how musicians feel about their work, why they get into the studios, and how they come to grips with their job contingencies.

During the last decade, the sociological literature dealing with field methods and interviewing has increased in self-consciousness as well as in sophistication. The contribution of these sections is intended not only to inform the reader of some of the ways in which this study was done, but more generally to supplement the current interest in research methods.

CONCEPTUALLY GUIDED SAMPLING

Any systematic random sampling of these players was impossible because the actual size and composition of the universe was uncertain. No complete listing of free-lance musicians working in the studios, for example, was available and only a very rough estimate could be made concerning the actual number of players who were called for available recording jobs. Defining who was to be interviewed could not, therefore, be done *a priori*. Such decisions had to follow the early exploratory field work. The American Federation of Musicians Local 47 Directory listed over 17,500 members in 1966. My guess is that approximately half or around 8,000 of these persons earn a substantial income from music.

Taking the size of the studio orchestras during the contract days as a rough indicator of the number of musicians in the motion picture and television film area alone (they naturally overlap with other free-lance work, such as phonograph recordings), we get the following breakdown: Fox, 50; Universal, 36; Warners, 50; MGM, 50; Paramount, 45; Columbia, 36; and the independent studios around 100 musicians. This included various players not on contract but called to do studio work on a steady basis during these years. This adds up to 360. This is under five per cent of 8,000 in the Directory. Within the 360, I located a group of "inner circle" or preferred players which narrows to about 190 (see below). Let us briefly note how this sample developed from the early interviews.

In my first four interviews I talked to established musicians at one of the major film studios. Statements were made by these respondents, two string and two brass players, about the fact that some of their colleagues were busier than others. Some were said to be, in their words, "at the top of studio work" "the guys who work all the time," or conversely, "those who are a cut below the top," "hard-hit by the business." One cello player suggested that there was "a relatively small nucleus of musicians doing about 90 per cent of the work in town."

Following such invidious comparisons, I developed an approach which is basically a reputational technique applied to a specific segment of this occupation.[1] It involved asking our respondents to identify the "busier musicians in town . . . those in the top group." After ten interviews I had begun to compile a list of those players "on call" at the various studios. At this stage roughly three out of five respondents named essentially the same group of musicians; contacts were made with these people and interview dates were arranged. These reputational questions were asked of half of our total sample of 73; by this point (N=36), there were few names being added to our list of "top players" and these questions were subsequently omitted from the interview.

In my sampling procedures consideration was given to the instrument a musician played. This was done for the following reasons: (1) Work problems and more generally the work roles are different by instrument. Strings are essentially ensemble-coordinative roles while brass, woodwind, saxophone, and percussion are more individualistic, the latter musicians' performances being more audible. Furthermore, scores differ in the kinds of instruments needed; thus some kinds of instrumentalists might find more work than others depending on what type of "sound" is fashionable, as well as economical. (2) I reasoned that instrument played should have important implications for the musician's aspirations and career history. According to Samuel Antek's discussion of orchestra musicians, string players aspire to be concert artists

1. On the whole, and due to the relatively small number of musicians in the inner circle, there was general consensus as to who were the busiest players. This procedure for identifying and then interviewing is developed by Floyd Hunter, *Community Power Structure* (Chapel Hill: University of North Carolina Press, 1953).

while brass and woodwind instrumentalists aspire to, and are more satisfied with, an orchestral career. (Support for this interpretation can be found in Chapter 3.)

"The musicians who make up our larger orchestras are a mixed group with varied personalities, backgrounds, and skills. They may be divided most simply into two groups; the wind players and the string players. In training, achievement, and musical outlook, these two groups differ greatly. Everyone who studies a wind instrument professionally accepts the facts that he will end up playing in an orchestra. String players are different. There is hardly a string player in a major symphony today, with the exception of brass players, who did not turn to the orchestra as a last grudging, desperate concession to economic necessity. To the string player, a symphony orchestra offers little opportunity for personal expression or artistic creativity of his own. By and large, he resents the personal tyranny and artistic abuse of conductors. Like geisha girls who dance for whomever pays them, orchestral musicians play to suit the taste and musical whim of whomever they play for, and their every musical instinct may be violated in doing this. They are in no sense self-expressive artists. Eventually they become only skillful automatons, giving no more, no less, than they are forced or cajoled into giving. As their original enthusiasms become dull and jaded, music-making itself becomes a monotonous grind, and playing in a symphony orchestra but another way to make a living, one far removed from the dreams and desires that prompted the grueling work required to master an instrument. Many musicians in large symphony orchestras actually grow to hate music and music making."[2]

The final sample of musicians consists of a group of high-ranking musicians in the free-lance system. Fifty-nine (or 81 per cent) of the final sample are players

2. Samuel Antek, *This Was Toscanini* (New York: Vanguard Press, 1963) pp. 71-74.

Table A.1

Instrument	1 Reputational Approach: Names within the "top group of musicians"	2 Total Interviewed of "top group"	3 Final Sample
Violin	20	8	14
Viola	11	1	3
Cello	15	5	6
Bass	14	3	3
			(26)
Tuba	4	1	1
Trumpet	23	5	5
Trombone	16	4	4
Sax-Doublers	25	8	9
Percussion-Drums	19	5	6
			(25)
Clarinet	9	4	4
Flute	9	5	6
Bassoon	6	4	4
Oboe	5	2	2
French horn	12	4	6
			(22)
Total	(188)	(59)	(73)

selected by their colleagues as being "among the busier players in commercial work."

The total sample is composed of 73 musicians. Table A.1 identifies the structural composition of the inner fraternity of free-lancers; these are the musicians contractors continually hire for motion picture, television film, phonograph, and jingle recording calls. They are the top entrepreneurial musicians for hire when a call goes out for their particular instrument. Moreover, those who constitute this reputational sample identify themselves as being in the "top group," thereby providing *subjective* proof of membership. The reader will notice that 19 per cent (N = 14) of the respondents were *not* identified by their colleagues as being the most in demand or in the "top group." While they are active in the studio recording scene, and some were members of studio orchestras during the contract days, they are farther down the contractors' lists. Some are breaking into film and recording work. In short, they are on the edge of what I have called the *inner circle* — the group of approximately 190 free-lancers. They play the following instruments: violin, 6; viola, 2; cello, 1; saxophone, 1; percussion, 1; flute, 1; French horn, 2.

Within the inner circle there is an even more highly select group of players. These free-lancers typically play the principal and second chair parts: in the brass and reed sections, the lead and solo parts; in the string sections, the concertmaster, first and second stand positions. They occupy the most privileged position within the orbit of the inner circle; they are the most highly in demand by contractors. Their incomes are typically the highest of all respondents. By my estimation, this exclusive orbit numbers around 80. They play the following instruments: violins, 7; celli, 5; violas, 3; bass, 10; saxophones, 15; flutes, 5; clarinets, 4; oboes, 3; bassoons, 2; trumpets, 10; trombones, 7; and French horn, 6.

In the "overall sample" there are 26 string players, 22 woodwind, single-reed and French horn players, and 25 brass- saxophone-doublers (sax plus another set of instruments such as clarinet, another saxophone, etc.), and percussion players. The instrument played, as noted, is associated with a particular type of organizational and/or musical setting. Strings, woodwinds and reeds, such as flutes and clarinets, and French horn are traditionally orchestral, chamber ensemble, or in the case of the violin and cello, solo instruments.

By way of contrast, saxophone, brass, such as trumpet and trombone, and percussion instruments are typically associated with either the orchestra, concert band, big dance band, or jazz setting. My comparisons on the basis of instrument revealed that the string musicians came largely from orchestra backgrounds, solo careers, and so did the woodwind and reed players. Brass, saxophone, and percussion players were largely from the big bands of the forties and the jazz field. Thus persons in the three categories differed not only in career backgrounds, but within each group there was consistency in career history.

The average age for all players was 46 years. The string musicians were slightly older (average age 47, range from 33 to 57). The brass, saxophone, and percussion players were slightly younger (average age 45, range from 29 to 52). Time of entry into studio work in Los Angeles for the entire sample was as follows: prior to 1946, 30 per cent; 1947 to 1951, 30 per cent; 1952 to 1957, 21 per cent; and from 1958 to 1966, 19 per cent. Slightly under 60 per cent of our musicians had worked during the studio contract period either on contract with a particular studio or as an independent free-lancer.

In terms of educational attainment and musical training, 31 performers had completed either a four-year college or conservatory instruction such as Julliard, Curtis Institute, Eastman School of Music, or various institutes in Europe. Three had Masters degrees; 15 had begun their education in a four-year college or conservatory but did not complete that training; 27 had finished high school or less.

Twenty-one players had spent three or more years in major symphony orchestras such as the Boston Symphony, Philadelphia Orchestra, Pittsburgh Symphony, Rochester Philharmonic, Seattle Symphony, and others. Sixteen of these persons had held principal or assistant principal positions in their respective orchestral sections during their careers. Since entering studio work, several had been offered positions in major orchestras. Nineteen musicians had worked three or more years in the big bands, such as those of Glenn Miller, Woody Herman, Claude Thornhill, Benny Goodman, Paul Whiteman, and other famous bands. Twelve of these respondents had played either the lead (first) or solo jazz "chair." The remaining players had worked less than three years in the orchestras, big bands, or as concert soloists before moving into commercial work in New York, Chicago, and Los Angeles.

The income for respondents in 1965, which included income from all types of free-lance employment, ranged from $7,000 to $62,000 with a mean income of $27,800 and a median of $26,000. Over 80 per cent of these players earned 60 per cent or more of their total earnings from work in the motion picture and television film area of free-lance work. The rest was divided among phonograph recordings, jingles, and other types of calls including outside "leisure employment" in chamber symphonies, recitals, jazz dates, and various "casual" calls. This figure suggests, quite independently of reputation, that I have selected a group of performers who are among the busiest musicians in this type of work. The mean income for the strings was $24,800 (a range from $16,000 to $48,000); for the woodwinds and French horns it was $22,095 (a range from $7,000 to $45,000); and for the brass, saxophone, and percussion players it was $36,167 (a range from $19,000 to $62,000). The latter figure reflects the fact that saxophone-doublers and percussionists usually receive additional pay for each extra instrument on a call.

THE METHODS

Musicians selected for the sample were contacted over the telephone and asked to cooperate with the study; they were told that the interview was part of a study of "the free-lance musician in Los Angeles" and that it would take about an hour. Interviews were conducted by the author from July 1966 until August 1967. In five cases I was refused an interview and in four other instances the musicians said they would call back but never did. Follow-up calls to these players through their answering services led nowhere. I tried for about five days, then gave up.

One problem appeared to be particularly salient for about a quarter of these musicians over the phone, and that was the issue of anonymity. I can only speculate about this, but it appears that free-lance work in Los Angeles gives rise to jealousy and a stress on politicking to get jobs. In a relatively small occupation, negative sentiments can be easily transmitted; hence, the outsider is treated with caution until he can establish himself as a person who can be trusted. Having studied trumpet with two eminent musicians in town helped, and my task became easier as potential respondents heard about the research from other musicians (who agreed to talk to them for me).

INTERVIEW SCHEDULE

Rather than to into a discussion of our individual items and their conceptual origins, I will briefly discuss the interview schedule in descriptive terms. My preference is to let the conceptual framework emerge in the substantive sections. The schedule was divided into several sections. First, the respondent was asked about his work history as a musician on a year-by-year basis. Of interest here was not simply an account of the settings and organizations in which he worked, but more generally a feel for the social and historical context in which his career developed. This not only helped in getting the interview moving, putting the respondent (and interviewer) at ease, but led naturally into several questions about how the musician got into the studios and about the steps that led to his present situation. Following this, I was interested in exploring the feelings the performers had about their careers ("In your mid-twenties, what did you see as your ideal future in music," "What did you want to be if everything went your way," "When you first entered commercial music, how did you feel," "Was it something you really wanted to do and did you regard it as temporary or what?") Next, I wanted to get some idea about the person's distribution of wages in the various types of free-lance work. This was followed by a set of open-ended questions about problems at work ("Is there any job security in the free-lance field," "Is the music any better in one area than another," What type of calls are interesting and why," "Does playing in the commercial setting use your skills and talents to their fullest advantage," "What are some of the major problems you face as a free-lancer," etc.).

I used no one type of interviewing "technique," rather, the approach varied with the respondent. The main effort was concentrated on fully understanding and assessing the content of the respondent's statements. My aim was to make them clear, plausible, and coherent. Equally important was a concern for the musician's feelings: the affect associated with a particular response. My rule-of-thumb technique was to have responses to specific items backed up by non-directive probes, and in most cases I would ask for concrete descriptions. The general procedure was to move from the general to the specific. The musician's descriptions of work and career were probed to assess interpretations of events, cognitive perspective, and concrete experiences. Typical probes ranged from "Can you give me actual instances of this from *your* experiences?" to brief paraphrasing and "Could you give me an example of what you mean?" or interjections such as "When is this likely to happen," or "How would you sum up the way you feel about. . . ?" Success in these efforts can only be judged by the description, analysis, and illustration. I should note that out of all the musicians interviewed only a few could be characterized as bland or dull. Most of them liked to talk about themselves; the majority were sophisticated and even eloquent in the way they expressed themselves, and most elaborated at length when probes were initiated.

The length of the interviews ranged from one to five hours and the average time was an hour and fifty minutes. I used a tape recorder in 46 cases (or 63 per cent of the total). Time and expense of tape transcription was one reason for not recording all of the interviews. The major reason was largely pragmatic; by the fortieth tape transcription I had, to my satisfaction, adequate description and interpretation of the musicians' work and career experiences.

Tapes were transcribed as soon after the interview as possible. These averaged thirteen and a half pages. In only two cases did the musician refuse to have the interview, or selected portions of it, recorded. With few exceptions, all the musicians were very cooperative. Many of them showed interest in the tape recorder; some suggested particular brands of tape to use, and a few even wanted to run the machine. My impression is that this device had no basic disruptive influence on the course or content of the responses. These respondents were familiar with tape equipment and were apparently at ease in its presence. This gave me considerable freedom in taping only select portions of the interview, necessitating my turning the machine on and off. In addition to the tape recorder, all responses were written on the interview schedule. These notes facilitated later coding of items.

The research strategy was eclectic. An effort was made to utilize two types of data collection and analysis

— qualitative and quantitative. The method of presentation
was to fully describe and illustrate the substantive issue at
hand and at times support the discussion with frequency
distributions of the musicians' responses along a con-
ceptually relevant item.

It is appropriate to note some of the limitations of these
procedures as well as their advantages. First, my sample
of commercial free-lance musicians is not representative
of any precisely known population of musicians. I do not
have the parameters of those working in Los Angeles.
This limits my ability to generalize to a wider population
of musicians. Second, my selection techniques were by no
means random. They developed as the research progressed and the occupational structure unfolded; they
were not determined *a priori*.

The strengths and advantages of my approach seem
twofold. In an effort to give a credible account of the
varieties of career and work experience, I discovered and
identified correspondence between variables which could
not be predicted beforehand on the basis of present substantive theories of commercial musicians or popular-culture work settings.

A second advantage pertains specifically to my ability
to generalize about musicians' work experiences. My
methodological interest, which is documented more fully
in the next section, was to get as close as I could to these
performers' actual concerns, perspectives, and feelings
about what they do for a living and to generalize about the
commonly shared perspectives of these performers. Despite the limitations of the sample, my claim is to have
identified on a general level certain recurrent and persistent career problems among performers working not
only in the commercial recording setting — in Los Angeles,
New York, and Chicago — but also in "legitimate" symphonies throughout the country.

Methodological Appendix B: Some Personal Reflections on the Research

This study moved through a number of stages, each with its own unique characteristic, each of which made its distinct contribution to the theoretical and methodological formulations which finally were developed. What began as an interest in the sociology of the performing artist working in an orchestral setting, guided by a few notions and a tentative research instrument, developed into a more complete examination of the work and careers of free-lance musicians working in the Hollywood film studios. The aim of this section is to set forth the basic outlines of the research and the problems faced at each stage.

Chronologically, the history of the study involved roughly the following phases: (1) initial explorations and pre-tests for a study of orchestra musicians, (2) some changes in the substantive area, respecifications of the interview items, and the emergence of several common-sense "models" of the actor, (3) my changing role as the research developed—from an "informed observer" to "inside dopester"—and further methodological difficulties, and (4) assembling the evidence, coding and editing the tape recordings and some notes on their use. My briefly describing some of these stages and their problems may benefit other investigators in the sociology of work, careers, or the arts by showing them the methodological problems encountered as well as some of the solutions developed.[1]

INITIAL EXPLORATIONS

This research began as a study of the work and careers of symphony orchestra musicians. My own background and training as a brass player, which included study with several symphony players, had naturally given me an interest in the sociology of the arts, particularly the performing arts. During the second year of my graduate study I began to see some of the implications a study of musicians would have for several areas of sociology. Westby's study of career experiences of orchestra members, Antek's insights into the problems of string players in symphonies, and several reports on the economic situation of the country's orchestras further stimulated my interest.[2]

1. William F. Whyte, *Street Corner Society* (Chicago: University of Chicago Press, 1943); Phillip Hammond, *Sociologists at Work* (New York: Basic Books, 1964); David Riesman's reflections in Paul F. Lazarsfeld and Wagner Thielens, Jr., *The Academic Mind* (Glencoe, Ill.: The Free Press, 1958); Charles C. Moskos, Jr., "Personal Remarks on Sociological Research in the Third World," in *Sociological Self-Images: A Collective Portrait,* edited by Irving Louis Horowitz (Beverly Hills, California: Sage Publications, 1969), pp. 101-116; Philip L. Newman, *Knowing the Gururumba* (New York: Holt, Rinehart and Winston, 1965); Gerald D. Berreman, "Behind Many Masks: Ethnography and Impression Management in a Himalayan Village," *The Society for Applied Anthropology,* Monograph No. 4, 1962; and Howard Becker, "Problems of Inference and Proof in Participant Observation," *American Sociological Review* 23 (December, 1958), 652-660.

2. See Baumol and Bowen's *Performing Arts: The Economic Dilemma* (New York: Twentieth Century Fund, 1966) for a detailed listing of the literature dealing with the economic state of the arts.

A proposal and interview schedule were drawn up during the summer of 1966; the aim was twofold. On the one hand, I wanted to describe and explain different career patterns, aspirations, and adaptations of orchestra musicians. And, on the other hand, I wanted to consider these career features as important factors in influencing a player's view of his work—his commitment to an orchestra, his work satisfaction, and evaluation of what he does.

My discontent with many studies designed to ascertain the "meaning" of work and work satisfaction certainly influenced the style of research that was to be undertaken.[3] I decided a tape recorder would be used in the context of a semi-structured interview. I had confidence in my ability to carry on conversations with musicians and, most importantly at this point, I thought the project would be fun to do. The interview schedule explored several aspects of the musician's work situation, his career aspirations, and work history. The idea was to obtain a musician's chronology of career aspirations much like Chinoy did in his study of automobile workers.

As a pre-test, I selected five musicians working in the motion picture and television film industries in Los Angeles—instrumentalists who, in the argot of commercial music, work "in the studios." They were selected for two reasons: (1) many of these players had come from symphony orchestras and thereby they gave me a chance to explore some of Samuel Antek's leads plus an opportunity to pretest some questions, and (2) in the Los Angeles area only one orchestra was available for my interviews. A pre-test with those players would necessarily limit the eventual number of cases. One of the members of my committee at that time was a free-lance studio player. He

3. See Blauner's "Work Satisfaction," and Mills' *White Collar,* *op.cit.* p. 229 for critique of the methodological limitations of work satisfaction studies.

provided me with many useful facts about the industry as well as the names of several players in free-lance work. He was also an important entree into the studio scene. During the summer of 1966 the interviews began.

It is commonplace to note that the preconceptions an investigator takes with him into the field—into the research situation—have important consequences. Probably more commonplace, but not as frequently noted nor documented, is the fact that first attempts in the field often ignore important distinctions, overlook others, and, in some cases, are just plain incorrect in respect to members' social reality.[4]

The problem immediately encountered was that my implicit, common sense typification of the performing musician (in this case both the symphony orchestra and commercial musician) borrowed someone else's rhetoric. I went into the field with essentially two types of performers in mind: the "frustrated artist" and one that might be termed the "commercial entrepreneur." The facile dichotomy, borrowed from the literature on "mass society," left me totally unprepared for the subjects I interviewed and the responses I received. I suspect that the humanists' distaste for the material world helped to produce this distinction between the conception of the artist found in Berlioz's writing[5] and that presumed to characterize intellectuals and artists who work in "mass-culture industries." What was troublesome was that I had been successful in concealing from myself this rather simple model of human nature, and the presumed impact of particular types of work on artists. Problems

4. Melville Dalton, *Men Who Manage: Fusions of Feeling and Theory in Administration* (New York: John Wiley and Sons, Inc., 1959), pp. 273-285.

5. Hector Berlioz, *Evenings in the Orchestra,* translated by Charles E. Roche, (New York, London: A. A. Knopf, 1929).

encountered in the early stages of the research led to a rethinking of my own preconceptions about the research, and the implicit assumptions I was building into the project at this stage. For example, following the leads of Antek, Westby, and Virgil Thompson, I was overlooking the *pragmatic* and often *prosaic* ways in which these respondents described their work. One saxophone player explained his views on his work in the following terms:

> You got to get a good sound on your instrument, you have to be able to play accurately and rhythmically correct. The qualifications are simple, really. You have to be proficient, to have those things second nature. Actually it's very simple. I think a lot of people try to put this into a very difficult, nebulous thing, and yet it isn't. You're learning your crafts, like a good plumber or carpenter would. Play with the guy next to you, play good, follow the man with the stick and do what he tells you to do, that's all there is to it.

I was starting with the wrong set of presuppositions about commercial musicians. I began with the question, "Are these guys alienated artists?" rather than with the more basic question, "What are the essential features of the work role, and what accounts for the differences in how they look at their work?" One musician went to some length to explain for me the meaning of the term "artist" to him.

> I would say an artist in this respect is where a person writes his own music and plays it. I don't consider Heifetz or these people purely creative people. They don't write the music, they just play what the guy wrote down and they play it very well; they knock you out. That's just my own interpretation of it. I consider myself a fine craftsman. They bring the music in and I play it, that's the way it has to be, play it *right now*, efficiently. Does that make sense?

And another:

> I guess I consider myself a studio musician, yes, but with reservation. I'm free-lance player and that covers everything

from jazz dates to the Hollywood Bowl, which is a wide variety. I don't think you would say studio musician, because this means to me X Studio and that's about it, but for me that isn't it at all.

When I asked one string player if his work was dull and monotonous all of the time he looked puzzled and then said:

All of the time? No, that's not right. It depends on the call: how much money the producer has for music, the amount of time put in on the score, the musicians you're working with. It's a difficult question to answer, I can't answer it.

At this point I was missing the changing nature of their work experiences and self-definitions as respectable craftsmen.

In exploratory research of this nature, I ran the risk of defining (and refining) a methodology more appropriate to one group than another. I also faced the possibility of becoming more interested in the individuals who composed my pre-test than those of the proposed study of orchestra musicians. One way of resolving this dilemma was to accomplish the aims of the pre-test and then move on to the original research objective. Another was to change the substantive area, reformulate the theoretical and substantive problem, and shift the perspective to accommodate the emerging interest. Implicitly, I had been following the latter course and was gradually getting interested in musicians working in the film area of free-lance employment.

In the early interviews, I found myself interviewing musicians whose careers ranged from the era of the great "big bands" to the outstanding symphonies in the country—including the famous NBC Symphony under Toscanini's direction. During the first ten interviews, I saw the opportunity to study the work and careers of a particularly unique group of performing artists; artists whose work was in an area of predominantly casual employment as well as within work settings assumed by many social critics of contemporary society to be the "mass culture industries" organized around a relatively unique production process.

But this was not the only consideration. Los Angeles, as the major capital of film production, not only possessed a unique free-lance situation but also facilitated my access to these musicians. I lived fairly close to several major film studios and literally minutes away from the San Fernando Valley and the western section of Los Angeles, areas in which the majority of musicians lived. This relatively unique setting and access to the industry, as well as the fact that this opportunity might not be available so easily in the future, influenced my decision to change the substantive area. Symphony orchestras, I reasoned, were located in the major cities of the country and, presumably, could be studied at any time. The film industry was close, the musicians were, so far, friendly, and the topic seemed sociologically important.

CHANGE OF INTEREST AND TURNING
POINT IN THE RESEARCH

I began to gather source material and information on the history and economic structure of the film studios, the free-lance musicians' work role, and the nature of the process of film production. Interest in the economics and "broader picture" of the industry led to writing up a section on the social and economic situation of the studios. This alerted me to the internal differences within the industry by studio and the close connection between musicians' earnings and the volume of motion picture and television film production. Source material from union records was useful in developing these ideas.

Interviews were conducted with several film composers and union officials to explore some of the features of free-lance hiring, composers' preferences for certain performers, and some of the work problems faced by composers. Contacts established here led to invitations to several film recordings. During these sessions I talked with the personnel in charge of sound reproduction and music editing, made notes on how the music was synchronized to the film reel, and chatted with musicians. On the hourly breaks I hung out near the coffeepot area or in other positions where I could overhear conversations between players.

In the open-ended questions, I wished to avoid the tendency of looking at attitudes towards work as *isolated bits of information.* My conception of work perspectives assigns a central place to the context of the musician's idealism and cynicism, as well as to the affect associated with these interpretations. I was more and more concerned with assessing (1) the various components which make up the work world of the respondent, (2) how these musicians describe their work, with contempt, annoyance, joy, ambivalence, or indifference, and (3) how career experiences shaped their views toward work. My interest turned to four conceptual areas — skill, control over hiring conditions, occupational status, and economic rewards — as they were reflected in the consciousness of the musician.

As the interviewing continued, I began to develop an interest in the different "types" of musicians interviewed as well as those mentioned during the course of the conversations. Internal differences within the occupation began to emerge as the project went along. What began as a set of leads and hunches about musicians I would encounter was gradually organized into a preliminary set of social categories. The categories that developed alerted me to different kinds of respondents within the free-lance work; they were also the first steps I made towards developing internal occupational comparisons.

The Utilitarian: Having broader musical goals beyond commercial work, this type of player sees his free-lance work in film and recordings as providing enough money so he can "do the things he really wants to do." These might include playing chamber music, touring, etc. Of concern to him is the opportunity for full utilization of his artistic skills and talents; he attempts to maintain a balance between making money and "art."

The Entrepreneur: This type is oriented towards his work almost exclusively in terms of its extrinsic features; the money in commercial work is his chief source of job satisfaction. Unlike the Utilitarian, he has few musical interests outside of making a living. His job satisfactions center around the chance for increased wealth and his typical job frustrations, if any, stem from the lack of desired economic rewards.

The Rate Buster: [6] Most talked about by other musicians and known collectively as "the most wealthy guys in the cemetary," "those guys with all the ulcers," "the guys who never turn down any work," this type, like his entrepreneurial colleague, is oriented almost exlusively towards the "business" value of commercial work. What differentiates him from the utilitarian and entrepreneur is his stronger adherence to a means-centered approach to his work. This type was most likely to talk about his "accounts" with contractors and "building up accounts" so he could do more work. The difference between Rate Buster and Entrepreneur is a matter of degree.

The Frustrated Artist: This type desired to be a concert artist, lead his own band, play principal desk in a symphony orchestra, or even make enough money in commercial music to launch a career in "art." He is frustrated because his move

6. Melville Dalton, "The Industrial Rate-Buster: A Characterization," *Applied Anthropology* 7 (1948), 5-18.

into commercial work was accompanied by a great deal of dissatisfaction and his aspirations were high. Unlike the utilitarian, the balance between "art" and "making a living in music" has not been achieved. His rhetoric is one of unattained ideals, dissatisfaction with commercial work, but also a lack of desire (or opportunity) to do anything about his present state. This type is often disposed to point out others like himself who ". . . look at themselves and wonder what the hell we're doing in this God-awful rat race." Unlike the utilitarian, an adjustment between early desires and later work has not been made. Unlike the entrepreneur and rate buster, this type is not disposed to "drive" himself to make a lot of money; though some become notorious Rate Busters ("look only towards the buck"), most do not. The dilemma, in any case, is between what he could have done and what he is now doing.

The understanding of these "types" was structured by common sense notions as to why musicians work in commercial music in the first place, what they bring with them into that setting, and some of the consequences that the setting would seem to have for them. Respondents also enjoyed gossiping and frequently a musician would point out that a certain musician felt a particular way about himself and his work; these were, however, merely rough characterizations of some of the differences within the occupation. Such common sense models served to direct attention towards two substantive concerns.

First, they illustrated the role of status evaluations in free-lance work. Musicians would frequently compare themselves with other players, making observations about their colleagues' volume of work (some being busier than others, some who don't work very much, etc.). From the sixth interview on I began to use such loose remarks as potential sources of valuable data. I began building up a list of respondents who were on call at the major studios by asking musicians to give me the names of the busiest players in town. Status evaluations and direct clues to the internal stratification of work emerged during the first five to ten interviews; for instance:

> It's no secret, we all know who the busiest players are, the guys most in demand. We also know who the best players, what their strong points are. . . .
> As you know there is a group of "all-stars" in town, they are called by most contractors, you want their names?
> I'd say about 100 players do the majority of work in film and recordings. One hundred players do about 90 per cent of the work, the *best work*.
> I'm not as busy as those in the swim of things.
> The union struggle in the late fifties was an attempt by the cream of the crop to control all the work in town.

My own "solution" to building up a sample was a compromise that restricted specific information about those musicians who were not the busiest (how many of them were there?) as well as limiting an attempt to get all the names of free-lancers outside the powerful core. This was the price I paid for focusing on the "inner-circle" of busy musicians. Nevertheless I did interview several musicians on the fringe of this group. This compromise was, however, in the line with the emerging research interest: the focus on a particular segment of the occupation.

Second, the types alerted me to the role that prior career experiences have on subsequent evaluations of work. I had several solid hunches that a musician's career would provide important sources of explanations for why he moved into commercial work and why he felt the way he did about it. As the "types" began to take form a few answers were suggested by the opportunities open to the musician when he entered the music business, his aspirations, the historical period in which he found himself, and some of the forces "pushing" him out of one setting into type of employment.

THE CHANGING ROLE OF THE INVESTIGATOR

Interviewing is an on-going process and requires that the investigator be aware of the transformations which occur in his own role. As the research moved along, I began to develop my common sense information about the respondents. This corresponded with a change in the way I was prepared to handle interview situations and looser conversations. I saw my presentation of self shifting from "newcomer" to "inside dopester." In the early stages I was learning as I went along. One of the difficulties with this was simply that I was asked for two types of information from the musicians: (1) regarding their career and work, the schedule called for respondent interrogation, while (2) at the same time I was implicitly asked for general information about free-lance film work, and thus the musician was also cast as informant while at the same time answering the interview questions.

As my knowledge and my skills as an interviewer increased, I was less reluctant to follow up answers which to me seemed vague or were susceptible to enlargement. One way of establishing who I was and how much I know was to display some previous knowledge. For example, when I indicated that I knew something about the informal organization of the occupation, or when I could show that others had given me a general idea of their income (". . . it generally ranges from $20,000 to $30,000 depending upon how popular you are, is that right" . . . "How about yourself?"), such familiarity offset my being defined as an outsider. My background as a musician undoubtedly helped in establishing rapport; and the more I interviewed, the more I could coerce respondents into giving detailed and frank answers. In general, if the musician knew that I already possessed some information, he was less likely to give vague responses or withhold details. Therefore, I could get to the essentials of an issue more quickly.

Aside from learning about the occupation, a major turning point in the history of the study coincided with the accumulation of a complete listing of musicians "on call" at the various studios and also with gaining access to and being accepted by a number of players who were the "busiest" in town, who formed an inner circle of top players. Establishing contact and making friends with them was helpful because they made further contacts with their colleagues easier. Sometimes the problem was simply trying to locate the musician through his answering service. Most of these musicians were extremely busy and for some it was easier to refuse the interview than to have their free time disturbed or to have to talk to someone during their meal between studio calls. One strategy helped: if I could inform the musician of the other musicians I had talked to, he was more likely to be interested.

As the interviewing progressed I had to warn myself against giving too much information while establishing "rapport" or using probes. In a few cases, the interview situation developed into a conversation. I reminded myself to stop being so polite and to get aggressive in eliciting information. In moving discussions to the level of musicians' concrete experiences, many demanded that I also be very frank. Here I warned myself not to tip my hand and inadvertantly disclose information that might influence my chance of interviewing other players or contractors. Some jealousy existed among players and during one interview, when the recorder was going, a musician expressed some resentment towards a few musicians, after which he began to get defensive. After more impoverished answers he reflected and said: "I shouldn't have mentioned those names, if they knew . . . well . . . let's just keep this whole discussion on a very general level, I'd rather not get into those politics, a lot of people don't like me and I wish you would turn off *that thing,* if any of this got around . . . "

The problem of knowing too much[7] points up the importance of the interviewer being aware of his changing role as the study progresses. In carrying on the open-ended probes, the "tell me more" stages, it is important that he be aware that the more he knows and the more he is "in the know" the more carefully he must guard himself against tipping his hand, getting too nosey or indiscreet in going after answers. Put simply, I warned myself not to wise up the respondent. This difficulty probably arises as the researcher becomes more self-confident and feels less need to act in ways which affirm his identity as the objective sociologist.[8]

After ten interviews I discovered I could profitably use the more diffuse conversations following the interview as potentially rich sources of information. Casual conversations after the tape recorder and clip board were put away seemed to provide the more informal and off-the-record type of situation. These conversations, in the living room or during the slow walk to my car, often led nowhere, trailing off into vague comments about the usefulness of the study. In other cases, respondents would begin to elaborate on something mentioned in the interview, pinpoint a particular dissatisfaction with their work, and even give names which they were reluctant to provide during the more formal interview setting. After completing these discussions and saying good-bye, I would get into the car, drive a couple of blocks and park, then write out detailed complete notes about what was said.

SOME NOTES ON EDITING THE TAPES

With the interviews completed and the tapes transcribed,

7. Dalton, *Men Who Manage, op. cit.*, pp. 283–284.
8. Blanche Geer, "First Days in the Field," in Phillip E. Hammond, editor, *Sociologists at Work, op. cit.*, pp. 372–398.

I had over 600 single-spaced pages of transcribed, recorded material, 50 pages of responses to particular items which were not recorded, and two notebooks of cross-tabs among the selected variables.

Files were assembled according to the following substantive areas: prior career history and background information, reasons for moving out, reasons for getting into commercial work, each component of work and the association between prior orientation toward and views of work. In an attempt to blend description and analysis, the sections on work were developed in order to give a credible account of what studio musicians consider to be the reality of their work circumstances and experiences, what they do, and what they feel they must do to perform their studio calls. I was interested in the commonly shared values of what is proper and efficient, and the relatively stable orientations to work tasks. Throughout, I wanted to place the particular into the overall setting with its inherent situational and structural exigencies. (The interview excerpts which appear throughout this study were chosen for representativeness, clarity, interest and verbatim accuracy. These responses are to be taken as representative of the majority of musicians unless otherwise noted.) On the quantitative side, codes were made of appropriate items and used to pin down the correspondence and frequency between variables. Within the limitations of the data, precautions were taken to formulate descriptive categories, discover possible links between variables, and develop a sense for the form and content of responses as well as refining my measurements as clearly as possible.

This style of research has obvious shortcomings, and I hope these brief reflections will alert the reader to some of them. More importantly this chronical indicates that researchers so inclined can carry out a design which involves considerable playing by ear while actively generating concepts and propositions, and continually assessing findings against an emerging conceptual framework.

Index

215

Printed in the United States
by Baker & Taylor Publisher Services